Dwellers All in Time and Space

Dwellers All in Time and Space

a memory of the 1940s

PHILIP OAKES

St. Martin's Press
New York

Library of Congress Cataloging in Publication Data

Oakes, Philip, 1928-
    Dwellers all in time and space.

    1. Oakes, Philip, 1928- —Biography. 2. Authors,
English—20th century—Biography. I. Title.
PR6065.A38Z463   1984   828'.91409   [B]   84-2064.
ISBN 0-312-22289-0

First Published in Great Britain in 1982 by André Deutsch Limited

First U.S. Edition

10 9 8 7 6 5 4 3 2 1

For my children again

Dwellers All in Time and Space

One

A GUST of wind blew the hat from my Uncle Percy's head and skimmed it over the snow bank buttressing the road and into the valley far below. Grains of ice pecked at his face and made his eyes water. His nose was scarlet as if it had been flayed. He held on to his hair with both hands and watched his hat cartwheel towards a small stream. 'After it, boy,' he shouted and I dropped my suitcase and plunged through the drifts in pursuit. The snow packed my shoes and stung my cheeks. I tripped over a submerged branch and tobogganed down the rest of the slope on my belly, coming to rest beneath a hawthorn, all the breath punched out of me. Somewhere behind me my uncle was still shouting, but the roar of the wind was gone and I heard running water and the tick of snowflakes foraging through the bracken. I rolled over on to my back and stared at the sky. It was pearly grey, the colour of the silk lining of my uncle's hat. When I turned my head the snow yielded like a pillow. I no longer felt cold. I wished I could stay there for ever.

It was late afternoon on a day in February. My uncle was escorting me to the Children's Homes which he and other relatives had decided was not only best suited to my needs, but properly punitive. I had shamed them all. The headmaster of the Bluecoat school in Wolverhampton which I had attended for the past four and a half years had demanded that I should be removed and I was in disgrace. Worse still, it was a humiliation I had inflicted on them all. Uncle Percy was himself a headmaster. My mother, widowed and an invalid, had been the headmistress of an infants' school. They were members of a large tribe; nine brothers and sisters, the children of a crate-maker in the

Potteries, who had advanced themselves socially and economically through hard work, and my conduct and disposition threatened the continuity.

I had committed no specific crime but I was, without doubt, a Bad Influence. The head of the Bluecoat school – a florid-faced singer who performed on the radio as George Gibbs, The Midlands Baritone – said so. My end of term reports were appalling. I was not stupid but indifferent, which was worse. I dodged games and I was once discovered loitering by the fire escape which led to the dormitories in the girls' wing. I was in no way a good example but my worst failing was my credulity. I believed rumours that money donated to finance a school outing to Dudley Zoo had been diverted to the headmaster's pocket, and naïvely repeated the tale in a letter to my mother. At the same time I let fall the news that I knew 'all about mastibation' and in her distress my mother showed the letter to her elder brother.

Uncle Percy's reaction was predictable. I had slandered a fellow teacher. The school should be informed of my moral turpitude and I should be made to face up to the consequences. Unfortunately, they were more drastic than even my uncle had anticipated. Mr Gibbs wrote to my mother more in anger than in sorrow telling her that I would be permitted to remain at school until the end of term, after which I was to take my permanent leave. There was to be no discussion, no appeal. Without regret I surrendered my uniform of blue cloak with its starched white cravat and black moleskin trousers with three silver buttons on each seam and beneath the dim dormitory light, put on the clothes my mother sent me from home. When I passed through the front door to catch the tram to the station the headmaster, who had been shaking hands with departing pupils, ostentatiously turned his back. We parted company in silence.

I was surprised by the turn of events and their abruptness, but I was not unhappy. I had friends who attended local schools and I assumed that in due course I would join them. No one contradicted me, although my mother said I must surely understand how difficult it would be for me to live at home. Six years previously a surgeon in Manchester had removed a tumour from the right side of her brain. Her life had been saved, but her left arm and left leg were now almost completely paralysed. She also suffered bouts of *petit mal*. 'My attacks,' she called them, refusing to name the epilepsy she thought so degrading. Once I entered her bedroom to find her on the floor, her eyes rolled back into her skull so that only the whites showed and a froth like that on freshly poured milk streaming from her mouth. She intended to protect me from sights like that, she said. It was no way for a boy to see his mother.

One morning I was dispatched to Dr Irving's surgery, ostensibly to collect a prescription and for what my mother described as 'a routine check-up' for my next school, wherever it might be. She handed me a sealed envelope to give to the doctor, licking the flap and ironing it shut with her fist with more vigour than seemed necessary. I walked down Macclesfield Street and through the park and when I reached the swings, dangling like gibbets in the winter mist, I opened the envelope and read the letter it contained. The single page bore the heading of the Children's Homes and I learned to my incredulity that I had been accepted for their branch in Lancashire the following month.

I was so angry I could scarcely breathe. There had been no hint from my mother or any other of my relatives that once again, I was to be sent away from home. There had been no warning. Plans had been made, letters had been exchanged, my future had been decided without anyone troubling to ask what I felt about the matter. I was hurt and I was insulted. My feelings and my opinions were worth nothing. I locked my arms about the chains of the swing and rocked myself backwards and forwards, watching the mist gather itself into brilliant beads on the sleeve of my jacket. There was a thick hedge of rhododendron between the playground and Moorland Road and I practiced a detachment which I knew would be necessary if I was to continue with the business of the day. I studied each bush in turn, imagining the green leaves, dull with soot, as the scales of a beast, a mythical familiar which I could summon up to rend and terrify all those who had abused me. I longed to believe in magic. I believed in nothing else.

Eventually I slid off the swing and walked on to the surgery. Dr Irving sounded my chest and peered down my throat. He was deeply tanned, with silvery hair and a moustache like a wedge of stainless steel. His shirts always smelled as if they had been ironed five minutes earlier and when he tilted my head to inspect my ears, I inhaled the fragrance of his skin like a chemist's shop, a blend of lavender soap and antiseptic. He made his usual joke. 'No aches and pains? No boils or blains?'

'I'm all right,' I said.

'No nasty rashes I should know about?'

I shook my head. 'There's nothing wrong with me.'

'Good, good.' He unscrewed the cap from his fountain pen and scribbled on a form on his blotter. 'Scabies,' he said to himself. 'You've never had scabies, have you?'

'No. Only impetigo.'

'Oh yes, I remember that. Very nasty.' He stroked his moustache, grooming the bristles with the back of his index finger. 'It's just routine. What we call a clean bill of health. Everyone demands that.' He signed the bottom of the form and blotted the signature. 'I spent yesterday examining soldiers,' he said. 'Conscripts rather. People wanting to dodge the column. You wouldn't believe some of the excuses.' He patted my shoulder. 'It's not your concern. Please God it never will be. How old are you now? Thirteen? It should all be over by the time you're needed.'

'I wouldn't mind,' I said.

He smiled indulgently. 'I'm sure of that. But it's not what we want. We want something better for you.'

I thought of what he had said as I walked home. It was 1941 and the war was into its second year. At the Bluecoat school we had grown used to air-raids. A bomb had fallen in the playing field opposite the school and the following day we had collected torn fragments of steel, one of them still bearing part of an inscription in yellow paint. It was strange to think of it being made in a German factory, hoisted into a bomb bay and falling through the night sky to gouge a crater in our football pitch. No one had been killed, but instantly the war had been brought closer in a way that broadcasts and newspaper reports had failed to do. Remotely we knew that the British Expeditionary Force had been driven from France, but the defeat was overlaid by the gallantry of the little boats which had plucked the troops from the beaches of Dunkirk. Later that summer the Battle of Britain entered our folklore. We kept tally of the planes destroyed in dog-fights over beaches and hop fields as eagerly as we noted county cricket scores. Our heroes were fighter pilots. Our favourite colour was RAF blue. Without difficulty I saw myself in uniform, a pair of wings tacked to my breast. But the combat I imagined was exhilarating and devoid of risk; the outcome certain. We knew we would win, whatever the setbacks. Everyone told us so.

My mother was less certain, although she had never admitted the fact until I demanded to know why she was sending me to the Homes in Lancashire. 'You'll be safer there,' she said.

'That's not the reason.'

'It's one of them.'

'I'm not going.'

She folded her hands in her lap. 'It's all arranged. I've filled in the forms. It's down there in black and white.' She brandished the envelope containing the document which Dr Irving had so casually filled in. 'We talked it over after you sent that dreadful letter. We decided it was for the best.'

'Who decided?'

'We all did. Your Uncle Percy made enquiries and he suggested the Homes. I'm not well enough for you to stay here. I've told you that often enough.'

'I wouldn't be any trouble.'

'You're nothing but trouble. You've let us all down.'

Her cheeks were flushed. Tears glinted in her eyes and I felt my own begin to smart in sympathy. It was important not to cry at this point. To do so would be to capitulate, to surrender before the actual engagement. I had learned to guard myself against my mother's weeping. If I managed to remain stony-faced for no longer than two minutes, her upset warmed to anger. She did not shed tears simply for effect, but if they were ignored she felt that she had made a gift of feeling which had been rebuffed. Injury was replaced by insult and the argument could then proceed. We were dangerously alike, aware of each other's weaknesses, alert to each other's tactics. It was difficult for either of us to devise a battle plan which the other could not anticipate. We were both ruthless, but I had learned the advantage in holding firm throughout the opening skirmish. It showed positive thinking. It emphasised the justness of my cause. To waver was to acknowledge that some vestige of right existed on the other side. I wanted my mother to admit that, whatever offence I had given, she had been vengeful and wrong in committing me to yet another institution.

'You went behind my back,' I said.

'I did what was necessary.'

'You could have told me what you were doing.'

'And start a row like this?'

'Is that what we're having? A row? I thought you were simply telling me why you told lies.' I felt the moral ground harden beneath my feet. The threat of tears had vanished altogether.

'What do you mean, lies? How dare you!'

'You did one thing and let me think another.'

'Rubbish!'

'You and Uncle Percy. Why should he decide what happens to me?'

'He's my brother and he cares about my welfare even if you don't.'

I shrugged my shoulders and thrust my hands deep into my trouser pockets. To show disrespect for my mother's family was the worst insult I could offer. I refrained from actual abuse, but there was no mistaking what I felt. My actions were as emphatic as any words I might utter.

'Don't be so rude,' she said.

I gave a snort of what I hoped sounded like contempt. 'I won't be here to be rude for much longer. You've made sure of that.'

'I'm not going on with this conversation,' said my mother. She turned her head violently and stared out of the window. I could bait her further, but there was no point. There was nothing I could say or do to change things. Arrangements had been made. I did not share my mother's reverence for the forms she had signed. But from past experience I knew them to be implacable. They signified that events had been set in motion and it was not in my power to call a halt.

Two weeks later my case was packed and I was sent on my way. Uncle Percy volunteered to be my escort, not to keep me company but to make sure that I arrived at my destination. The literature from the Homes had emphasised that there was no uniform ('You'll like that' said my mother) and that boys and girls lived separately in small family units. I put on my new green sports jacket and my first pair of long trousers and inspected myself in the wardrobe mirror. I felt dismally apprehensive and took refuge behind a flippancy which faltered the moment I saw my uncle warming his backside at the dining room fire.

'Time to be off,' he said, nodding at the clock whose chimes had aways reminded me when I awoke in the dark that I was at home and school was still at a safe distance.

I smiled brightly. 'Zero hour, you mean.'

'I mean exactly what I say.' He tightened his trousers across his buttocks and leaned back another inch towards the fire. My uncle was a tall, raw-boned man with the top joint missing from the little finger of his right hand and a beak of a nose that seemed to launch his face towards anyone he engaged in conversation. Even at his most amiable he had the air of being poised for attack.

'You'll not be too late back, will you?' asked my mother.

He sniffed loudly while he computed the vagaries of trains and buses. 'Late enough. And it's a beastly day for it.'

'Oh dear,' said my mother. 'I am sorry.'

My uncle chafed his hands as if he was trying to cram some extra warmth into them before leaving the comfort of the room. 'The forecast's not good. It's trying to snow already.'

'It's bound to be worse up there,' I said. 'Perhaps we'll have to turn back.'

My uncle sniffed again and shook his head. 'I'll deliver you. As promised. Never you fear.'

'It's so good of you,' said my mother.

'Someone had to do it,' said my uncle.

I stared mutely at the carpet and my mother dug me in the ribs. 'Say thank you,' she hissed. I hesitated and she nudged me harder still.

'Thank you,' I said.

'You mean thank you Uncle Percy,' said my mother.

My uncle raised his nose and regarded me down its great length. 'He'll learn better manners where he's going.'

'Oh dear,' my mother said again.

Trying to interpret her exclamation I decided it was not so much alarm for what awaited me as a reproach for my continuing ingratitude. Instinctively my mother supported authority. I had overstepped the mark by complaining about my headmaster and casting a momentary slur on his integrity. I had challenged her own motives and even now I was not showing the proper respect for my uncle. It was time that someone exerted the necessary discipline. She kissed me fondly, but with a measure of reserve. If I was going to the wars it was to be without any shedding of tears on the home front.

We caught the train from Stoke to Manchester. My uncle took a corner seat and engrossed himself in the *Times* crossword. Occasionally I caught him watching me over the

top of the newspaper. 'Here's one for you,' he said at last.
'Four down. Sad that great cricketer should be in this. Eight
letters.'

Through the train window I saw snow-patched fields
blurring together into seamless white and I pressed my face
to the pane to see what lay ahead. My uncle tapped my
knee. 'Did you hear what I said?'

'I don't know the answer. I can't do crosswords.'

'Everyone can do crosswords. All it requires is
concentration,' he said.

'I give up.'

'You've not even tried.'

'I don't feel like it.'

My uncle leaned forward and his nose hung over me like
a cleaver. 'There are times we all have to do things we don't
like. It's called putting up with it. Just bear that in mind.'

I was too dispirited to reply, but suddenly and
unannounced the answer to the crossword clue appeared
in my mind's eye like a message on a billboard.
'"Disgrace",' I said.

'What are you talking about?'

'"Sad that great cricketer should be in this."'

He sat back and studied his newspaper, then spread it in
his lap. 'You knew it all the time. Why didn't you say so?'

'I didn't know it all the time. It just came to me.'

'I don't understand you,' said my uncle. 'I don't
understand you at all.'

At Manchester we changed stations. There was sleet in
the wind and I saw a notice board on which there was a
chalked announcement warning that trains were running
late due to weather conditions. 'There's snow on the line,'
said a porter. 'There's men out there now with shovels.'

'We have to get to Bolton,' said my uncle.

'You'll be lucky,' said the porter.

My uncle sat me in the waiting room and went off to find
the station master. All the tears which I had not shed over
the past few weeks seemed to gather at the back of my
throat and rise effortlessly to spill down my cheeks. I

watched them patter to the floor, blending with the melted snow. A man wearing a cloth cap who was sitting opposite tapped me on the knee. 'Is he being unkind to you?'

I shook my head dumbly. 'You can tell me,' he said. 'There's no need to be scared.'

For a second I was tempted. There was a scary pleasure in the prospect of embarrassing Uncle Percy. But it was hard to predict where it all might end. I also found a comfort of sorts in giving way to my misery. It was an extravagance like spending all my pocket money at once, leaving myself with empty pockets which only luck or ingenuity would fill again.

The man in the cap poked the waiting-room fire and raised the poker menacingly. 'Is he your dad?'

'My uncle,' I said. 'He's taking me to school.'

'Where's that then?'

I blew my nose and composed myself. 'Edgworth. The Children's Homes.'

'Past Bolton?'

'I think so.'

There was a general shaking of heads. 'They've been snowed in for a week,' said a woman clutching an oilskin shopping bag. 'They're right on the moors. You'll never get up there today.'

The windows of the waiting room were coated with green paint in observance of the blackout regulations and criss-crossed with strips of sticky brown paper. This was supposed to lessen the effect of flying glass in the event of an air raid. We peered at each other through the gloom which blurred the room like a giant thumb, smudging the light and damping down the fire. When my uncle returned, stamping his feet and blowing on his hands, it was as if he was a courier from another country. Beads of condensation hung from his eyebrows and a drop at the end of his nose flashed like a diamond.

'There's a train in five minutes,' he announced.

'Have they cleared the line than?'

'Obviously, or we couldn't proceed.'

'There's no call to be sarky,' said the man in the cloth cap.
'The lad asked a civil question. Can't you see he's upset?'

'Upset?' Uncle Percy aimed his nose in the general
direction of the questioner. 'What do you mean, upset?
What's he been saying?'

'Nothing you wouldn't know already.'

A surge of disapproval thickened the gloom which
lapped us in the tawny twilight. 'You'll not get past Bolton,'
said the woman with the shopping bag. 'They've been
snowed up there for a week past.'

'My information is otherwise,' said my uncle.

The man in the cloth cap spat into the grate. 'Happen
they don't know it all. There's drifts up there like bloody
mountains.'

'There's no need for bad language,' said my uncle.

It was the tone of voice he used when addressing his
more obtuse pupils and it was a mistake. The man in the cap
rose smartly to his feet and took one step towards my uncle.
'Don't you tell me what's bloody needed,' he said. 'Coming
in here all la-di-da. Taking no notice when you've got a lad
crying his eyes out.'

Uncle Percy flinched but stood his ground. He was
nervous, but I remembered that as a headmaster he
frequently had to cope with irate parents. He brandished
his handkerchief and mopped the end of his nose. 'I
understand your feelings,' he said more reasonably. 'They
do you credit. But it's not as simple as that. Believe me.' He
seized my arm and hoisted me to my feet. 'This boy, my
nephew, is a trial to his family and a very accomplished liar.
He was expelled from his last school and he is on his way to
another where we hope he will learn some regard for the
truth. He is crying because he feels sorry for himself. There
is no other reason.' He squeezed my arm. 'Tell the
gentleman,' he ordered. 'Were you or were you not
expelled from your last school?'

I nodded silently and felt the sympathy ebb away. 'He
has not been ill-treated,' said my uncle. 'On the contrary.
He has been exceptionally lucky in having friends and

relatives who concern themselves with his welfare.' He polished his nose again and stuffed the handkerchief into his pocket. 'Now we must catch our train.' He raised his hat to the woman with the shopping bag and turned me firmly towards the door. 'Platform five,' he said. 'And look sharp about it.'

I did not look back. I hurried towards the train, my uncle panting behind me. We passed the guard who waved us on with his green flag. 'All aboard for the Northern Flier,' he shouted. 'Snowmen travel half price.'

I was pushed into a compartment and heard the door slam. The station slid away and within minutes we were crawling over a polar landscape, hump-backed with sheds, in which factory chimneys stood like trees in an endless forest, their north flanks powdered with snow. We burrowed into mist which flattened itself against the windows when the train staggered to a halt, flowing back when we jolted on once again. My uncle sat in his corner seat with his hat pulled down over his ears and his coat collar turned up. Pools of melted snow surrounded his galoshes. He had said nothing since leaving the waiting room and when he spoke it was only to reproach me further.

'Not only a liar but a sneak,' he said.

'No I'm not.'

'Letting down your family, hob-nobbing with anyone who'll listen.'

'It wasn't like that,' I said. 'They asked me if you were being unkind.'

'And am I?'

'I didn't say you were.'

'I should hope not.' His coat seemed to shroud him completely. Only his nose emerged from the tunnel of tweed, a raw protuberance, dewy at the tip, the colour of freshly sliced bacon. His voice was much hoarser than when we had started out and although he sounded as testy as ever his reproaches were more languid than snappish. Perhaps he was sickening for something, I thought, and immediately felt more cheerful.

At Bolton I was sent to enquire directions and we walked the half-mile to the bus station, my case dragging my arm out of its socket, an icy wind smacking our faces. We were the only passengers on the bus and the conductor warned us that if the snow was as bad as had been forecast we might not be able to proceed as far as the Children's Homes, which was where the bus normally turned to make the return journey. 'I'll have to charge you full fare, though,' he said. 'It's too much of a muddle otherwise.'

At Edgworth village both he and the driver got out of the bus and inspected the road. 'It's no good,' said the driver. 'The ploughs haven't got this far. We'd never get up that hill.'

We followed his gaze and saw a track climbing endlessly towards moors that stretched like glaciers beneath a torn sky. 'You'll have to leg it,' said the conductor. 'It's about a mile and a half.'

My uncle pointed his nose the way we were to go and without another word we set off. I felt the wind like fists against my chest trying to force me back. The track disappeared beneath fresh snow and I found myself stumbling along the top of a submerged hedge. There was not a house in sight. Trees bent their backs along the skyline. I marched on like Captain Scott, looking for signs of life. Behind me I heard my uncle shouting, the words plucked away by intermittent gusts and flung over my head like missiles. I turned to try and catch one of his dispatches and it was at that moment that his hat blew off and I slid down the bank while giving chase.

Breathless, I watched snowflakes rinse through tussocks of grass and drown themselves in the stream and thought how absurd it was that all the ambitions and upsets, the family plotting and the melancholy journey north should end here. My life up to this point had been deleted and I was required to start again. It seemed as good a place as any.

My uncle's hat was caught in a tangle of branches a few yards away, riding at anchor on neat little waves which had carved a channel through the snow. It was very peaceful. There was a smell of earth and decaying leaves, odours which lay in a seam below the level of the wind. A blackbird stabbed at a cluster of hawthorn berries and a greenfinch, as vivid as moss, waited his turn.

'Where are you, boy?' shouted my uncle and I picked up his hat and climbed back to the road. His thin grey hair was standing on end and his expression was desperate.

'We're lost,' he said, 'completely lost.'

'We can't be,' I said. 'We just have to follow the road.'

He put on his hat and tied it into place with his scarf. 'But where *is* the road?' he demanded. His voice was quite drained of energy and it occurred to me that he imagined himself derelict and frozen in some country ditch while, far away, his grief-stricken wife prayed for his return.

It seemed the right moment for a dash of the moral uplift so much favoured by my family. 'You know what my mother says?' I reminded him as we struggled up the hill.

'What's that?'

'She always tells me to keep on keeping on.'

He grunted and tightened his scarf.

'D'you think she's right?' I persisted.

'Probably.'

'She says I should keep right on to the end of the road.' As a matter of fact, she usually sang it. Harry Lauder, at his most homely, had always been a favourite of my mother.

My uncle did not reply. His breathing was laboured and the drop on the end of his nose was smeared over his upper lip like pale varnish. We turned a bend in the road and the Homes lay ahead of us. We stumbled on past several large houses towards what seemed to be the centre of the complex. There was a long wall like a fort, with portholes along the top of it and a great stone arch in the middle. On the near side of the arch there was a green painted door with a brass plate set in the wall. My uncle peered at it and read aloud: 'Edward Buller. Governor.'

He rang the bell, wheezing like a spent horse, and stamped his feet on the freshly swept steps. 'At least we're here,' he said. 'I imagine they'll put me up for the night.'

He imagined wrongly. Mr Buller was a pink, vigorous man with hair the colour of butter which he parted precisely in the middle. He was exceedingly jolly and became even more so when my uncle described our journey through the drifts.

'That's nothing,' said Mr Buller, peering through his window towards the moors which were now completely obscured by dark scudding clouds. 'It gets much worse than this. In fact I think we're in for a blizzard. I wouldn't hang about too long if I were you. People have been marooned for days.'

My uncle sipped a cup of tea and stared at the fire in the governor's grate. 'Is there somewhere I could stay?' he enquired, his voice purged of its usual assurance.

'No facilities here, I'm afraid,' said Mr Buller happily.

'The village perhaps.'

'I very much doubt it. They're not used to visitors.'

He put down his cup and stroked his rosy chin. 'Bolton's your best bet. There'll be one more bus this afternoon. That is, if they're still running.' He chuckled as if he found the alternative vastly amusing.

My uncle's trouser-legs steamed in the firelight and I felt a twinge of sympathy. He looked so old, so helpless beside the vitality of Mr Buller. I knew what he was thinking. They were both teachers, but they did not belong to the same race. The fraternity was more varied than my uncle had imagined. His reputation, his authority counted for nothing here. They shared no common ground. They inhabited different worlds.

'Right then,' said Mr Buller, clamping his hand on my shoulder. 'Time to say goodbye. We don't want your uncle missing his bus.'

I put my lips to my uncle's haggard face but he scarcely noticed. He was visualising the drifts ahead, the dimly lit trains and the icy platforms that lay between him and his bed. 'Thank you, Uncle Percy,' I said. My mother would have been proud of me, I thought. I had remembered my manners.

Two

THE NEXT MORNING I awoke to find someone kicking the foot of my bed. I looked up apprehensively and saw a squat, sturdy man with bright blue eyes standing over me. He wore a striped flannel shirt secured at the neck by a collar stud and a black waistcoat traversed by a gold watch chain. His arms were folded and his right hand supported the bowl of a pipe from which a blue thread of tobacco smoke climbed towards the ceiling. His posture implied that he had been waiting there for some time and that his patience was wearing thin. 'All right,' he said, 'let's be having you. Time to rise and shine.'

His name, I recalled, was Mr King. I had met him and his wife the previous evening when Mr Buller had steered me along the rutted road and through the front gate of Mosscrop House. 'Mr King is in charge here,' he said. 'He's what we call the Labour Master.He makes sure the important jobs get done.'

It was a flattering but not, as I discovered later, a wholly accurate description of Mr King's occupation. As Labour Master he was in charge of the casual work force of boys who had left school but had not yet been apprenticed to a regular trade. The jobs for which they could eventually train were limited to those essential to the running of the branch, but competition was fierce. There was a farm, a bakery, a boot-repairers, a smithy (which also offered a grounding in electrical repairs) and the branch stores. Only a few boys were accepted as apprentices. The rest joined Mr King's labour squad which was known as the Shop. They were responsible for sweeping the roads, moving furniture, spreading manure, mending walls, chopping firewood, clearing fields of sunken stones and laying the drains which would make them fit for farming. Everyone served time on the Shop. Older boys who were still at school were required to donate their Saturday mornings to community service. Juniors were press-ganged when rain threatened the hay crop or potatoes were to be planted or picked. There was no pretence that there was dignity in the labour. The work was there to be done and the chief art lay in doing as little of it as possible. I learned this in the months to come. I also came to appreciate the fathomless sloth that lay behind Mr King's busy façade. But my first impressions were very different.

As he stood by my bed I studied his face, pricked by pores as deep as dimples. He was going bald and his scalp showed pallidly between the watered strips of hair that spanned his head, linking ear to ear as if he was wearing head-phones. He had a large but firm belly and trim dancer's feet. His arms were furred with fine, almost invisible hair and they were as thick as the legs of pork which Mr James, our butcher at home, attacked so fiercely with his chopper. He seemed to be lost in thought, but without warning he gripped the edge of my bed, straightened his arms and tipped me to the floor. Deliberately he took the pipe from his mouth. 'When I say move, lad, move.'

I pulled on my clothes and followed the rest of the pack downstairs into the dining room. The chairs were stacked on the tables and most of the boys were on their hands and knees, hunched like jockeys, and scooting backwards in bursts of furious energy as if they were running a race in reverse. Each of them was kneeling on a felt pad, clutching a bundle of rags with which he burnished the floorboards. Each boy made several runs up and down his individual strip, applying polish from a large tin half-filled with orange wax and rubbing it off so fiercely that the oak planks glittered beneath his hands. I smelled pipe smoke behind me and turned to see Mr King leaning against the door, his legs elegantly crossed beneath his snug belly, his arms folded as before. 'We have no gentlemen here,' he said, apparently addressing no one in particular. 'There's only working lads in this house.'

A small boy with red hair so severely cropped that it looked like a rash showed me a locker where the rags and polish were kept. 'Help yourself,' he said.

I found a rag and went to work. Mr King sauntered over to watch me and when I glanced up I saw his belly looming over me like a thunder cloud. He puffed on his pipe. 'Don't use so much polish. Just dab it on the floor and work it in. It's elbow grease that counts.'

I tried to follow his instructions but my polishing rag was glazed with wax and left smears on the yellow boards. 'Rub harder,' said Mr King.

My heart pounded in my chest and sweat ran into my eyes. I could see myself shunting up and down my strip of floor until my hands wore holes in the rag. I examined the surface for smears and when I found none I looked up hopefully.

Mr King pointed with the glossy toe of his shoe. 'What's that?'

'A stain,' I said. 'It's in the wood.'

'Is it now?' He reached down to the offending spot and scooped up a thin rind of grease on his fingernail.

'I'm sorry,' I said.

'It's no good being sorry. Learn to do it right.'

I bent my back and polished the strip again. 'We've tamed tigers here,' said Mr King.

'I beg your pardon.'

'Tigers,' he repeated. 'We've tamed worse than you.' He pointed to a regimental badge tattooed on his right forearm. 'Ten years light-heavyweight champion of the British Army in India,' he said as if he was reciting his name and number. 'Undefeated. Never took a count.'

I was properly impressed. 'We did boxing at my last school.'

'Would you take me on then?' demanded Mr King.

'Not likely.'

Mr King unflexed his arm and put his pipe back into his

mouth. 'Right you are. Do as you're told. Pull your weight and don't get above yourself.'

It was more than a pep talk, I realised. Mr King was defining limits, warning me how I might transgress and advising me that I was under observation. Evidently I was considered a hard case, and I remembered my mother and my uncle filling in forms which they hid when I came into the room and which I had subsequently failed to intercept. In their eagerness to feed the archives they had provided me with a reputation which it would have been perilous to live up to. I resolved there and then never to come into direct conflict with Mr King.

He walked up and down my strip of the floor. 'That's more like it. Now go and get washed. Shirt off and don't forget to do behind your ears.'

In the washroom a line of smaller boys filed past a woman wearing a blue silk dress with a starched white collar. Her name was Sister Aggie and with Mr and Mrs King she shared the running of Mosscrop House. As I already knew from the pamphlets with which my mother had been supplied, the Homes were largely financed by Methodist chapels and organisations. There were thirty branches situated all over the country. There was an average of ten houses to a branch and each of them was staffed by women known as Sisters whose job was to act as house mother to small family units of boys or girls. It was not a religious order to which they belonged, but their uniforms and titles somehow set them apart. They were like nuns or wardresses; agents of the institution. Usually two of the Sisters were responsible for the management of a house but Mosscrop, as I had already been told, was where they tamed tigers. It was where the hard cases were subjected to the proper discipline and Mr King was the disciplinarian.

Sister Aggie had a flushed and fleshy face and small eyes which were miniaturised still further by the thick lenses of her spectacles. Her hair straggled from a loose bun and she had a faint but perceptible moustache. After we had washed and dried ourselves we presented ourselves for her inspection, baring our wrists and necks to show they wore no tidemarks. She pored over our flesh as if searching for a text which would miraculously surface the longer she looked, but she avoided touching us except for the very smallest boys. She seemed to be in a flux of embarrassment and irritation, tossing her head so that her glasses glinted and her hair spilled over her collar. When it was my turn she peered so closely that I felt her breath graze my naked back. 'Your neck's dirty,' she announced.

'Where?' I tried to see myself in the mirror on the wall.

'There.' She prodded me with her finger.

'I can't see anything.'

'Well, I can see it,' she said. 'There's muck you could grow turnips in.'

I sensed everyone watching me and while I tried to frame a retort Mr King sauntered into the washroom. 'Any bother, Sister?' he enquired.

She smoothed back her hair and lodged her glasses more securely on her nose. 'No, not really.'

Mr King propped himself comfortably against the wall while I scrubbed my neck with a flannel and then offered the glowing evidence to Sister Aggie. 'That's better,' she said. 'Now you can get dressed.'

'And look sharp about it,' said Mr King. 'It's breakfast in two minutes.'

Mrs King said grace. The boys sat at four long tables, two at each end of the room, while she shared a small central table with Mr King and Sister Aggie. She was small and pale with a drooping mouth and bags like purses of lilac silk beneath her eyes. She looked as if she had slept badly and the teacup was too heavy for her frail hand. When she buttered a square of toast she studied it for a full minute, then put it gently to the side of her plate. Sister Aggie refilled her cup and she sipped the tea reproachfully as though it was medicine which she was forcing herself to drink.

The previous evening when I had been brought to the house by Mr Buller we had been shown into the sitting room where Mrs King sat on a low nursing chair, an embroidery frame in her lap. Mr Buller traced the design with his finger. 'Roses again, I see,' he said.

'The wife's very fond of roses,' said Mr King.

Tapestries draped over the backs of two easy chairs confirmed his observation. They swarmed with red roses and yellow roses. There were even one or two blue roses.

'Does your mother do embroidery?' Mrs King asked me.

'She can't. She gets headaches.'

Mrs King threaded a needle with green silk and drew it through the canvas. A leaf budded beneath her hand and she smiled sympathetically. 'Your mother misses a great deal. You must be a good boy for her sake.'

'And for his own,' said Mr Buller. 'He must make his mind up about that. No more wasted opportunities.' He clapped me on the back. 'Go and make yourself known to the other boys.'

I did as I was told. They sat in a semi-circle around a small fire in the next room and I noticed that although several of them were bigger and I presumed older than me, all but one wore short trousers. The firelight bounced off their bare knees. 'She'll have them off you,' said a boy whose hair stood up from his head in Vaselined quills.

'She'll have what off me?'

'Them.' He plucked my trouser-leg. 'Only the biggest lads wear longies here.'

'My mother bought these,' I said.

They snickered silently at the fire as if I had said something amusing. 'I'm telling you,' said the boy with spiky hair. 'You'll be back in short pants tomorrow.'

'Happen he will and happen he won't,' said another boy. He wore a school blazer with a badge on the breast pocket. 'Where are you from?' he asked me.

'Stoke on Trent.'

'That's what I heard,' he said. 'Like me. Best place on earth. Where exactly?'

'High Lane. Near Burslem,' I said.

'Posh, are you?'

I shook my head. 'Not a bit.'

'Went to a posh school, though. That's what they say.'

I was suddenly aware that everyone present knew my entire case-history and I was being studied to see whether I measured up to it. 'I was expelled,' I said.

'What for?'

'I was a bad influence.'

'What's that?'

'You'll have to ask them,' I said. 'They just wanted to get rid of me.'

'Did they whack you there?' asked the boy in the blazer.

'Sometimes.'

'With a cane or a strap?'

'A cane,' I said. 'On the hand.'

'How many?'

'It varied. Six mostly.'

'They gave me a dozen once,' he said, spreading his palms for inspection. 'Six on each hand.'

'What for?'

'Smoking,' he said. 'How about you?'

I showed them a packet of Park Drive. 'Where can we have a drag?'

'In the furnace room,' said the boy with spiky hair. 'After tea when they've all settled down.'

The boy in the blazer held out his hand. 'My name's Ray Clutton,' he said. 'Come and sit next to me. Potteries lads should stick together.' He folded my fingers over the packet of cigarettes. 'Put them away, for Christ's sake. You don't want everyone to see what you've got.' He looked fiercely round the watching faces. 'And there's not room for all of you in that furnace room. Doss and Spiff and Skelly. That's the lot.'

Doss was dark and thick-set. Spiff was the boy with the spiky hair and Skelly was tall and abnormally thin. His knuckles stood out on his hands like knots of red amber and his eyes glared as if unseen thumbs were pressing them from behind. Other than myself he was the only one wearing long trousers. They were made of some dark worsted material which looked exhausted as though it had been repeatedly boiled and wrung out.

'Batley shoddy,' he said, intercepting my gaze. 'That's what they call it. Cheapest stuff on the market. It's for working togs mostly.'

'Not like this,' said Ray, fingering my flannels. 'You'll get all the lasses with these. They like a bit of swank.'

We shared a table for tea – slices of brown bread and margarine with one small green apple apiece – and afterwards I was led across the yard to the furnace room. It was cramped and dusty, like a shoe box stood on end. Skelly wedged the door shut with an iron rake. The furnace glowed and the wind sang in the chimney. I handed round the cigarettes and we all lit up. There was a concert of deep and dramatic inhalations.

'You want to keep it down as long as you can,' said Ray. 'That's how you get the benefit.' When he exhaled, his breath revealed practically no trace of smoke. 'It's all gone into the system,' he explained.

I thought about Mr King and his large, inquisitive nose. 'Won't they smell it on us?' I asked.

Ray delayed answering until he had digested another lungful of smoke. 'He's not bothered about us. Not so long as we don't make a show of it. He's an idle bugger.'

'Just do as you're told and look busy,' said Spiff. 'He told us that himself.'

'Army rules,' said Doss.

'He don't want no trouble,' said Skelly. 'He keeps telling us not to rock the boat.'

I learned that Skelly worked in the branch stores, distributing groceries to both the girls' and boys' houses. Doss was still a pupil at the branch school, but about to become apprenticed to the smithy. Spiff worked in the bakery and Ray attended a technical school at Bury. 'They'll send you out too,' he said confidently. 'Old Buller likes to show off his bright lads.'

After breakfast the next morning there was no sign of a bus and Ray and half a dozen other boys and girls set off through the drifts to the nearest railway station to wait for trains to take them to school. The rest of us were lined up in the dining room. One of the smaller boys handed out hymn books and in a double column we marched off to assembly. Mrs King stood at the dining room window and watched us go, her eyes like bruises in her pale face.

As we crunched over the rutted ice I saw that the branch was like a small village. The governor's house was its centre and facing it across the road was the administrative block, flanked on either side by the dairy and the laundry. Another block further down the road housed the stores and the kitchens with the bakehouse in the basement. The assembly hall was next to the school and behind it, the playground was ruled off from the moors by a low drystone wall. Buried among the buildings there was also a large garage where tractors were repaired and, further up the road towards the athletics ground, there were the flower and vegetable gardens. Cabbages stood in close order beneath the snow. A twist of smoke streamed from the chimney of the potting shed. Solitary birds flapped across the sallow sky.

Morning assembly was brief. House by house, the boys gathered on the right of the hall. Girls assembled on the left. At the end of each row stood a house sister, ready to intercept any message or glance from the opposite side. Mr Buller read the lesson and offered a prayer. We sang a hymn. There were several terse announcements dealing with choir practice, the stacking of milk crates and the need to conserve food. We sang another hymn and then, row by row, we filed out into the playground.

I was taken in hand by Doss. 'You'll need to see Buller to find out what class you're in,' he said. 'Not that you'll be here long.'

'Why not?'

'Like Ray said, he likes to show off his bright lads. He'll pack you off to grammar school in a month or two.'

A group of girls standing in a circle behind us burst into shrieks of laughter as I pulled on my gloves.

'What's wrong with them?' I asked.

'Daft lasses,' said Doss. 'They're trying to get off with you.'

'How's that?'

He sighed as if the explanation was too obvious to need spelling out. 'None of us lads wear gloves. They're letting you know about it.'

I lifted each hand in turn and smoothed the leather over my knuckles. A girl with a red scarf knotted about her throat stepped forward from the group and imitated me. Her hair was the colour of milk chocolate and pulled back smoothly through a rubber band. She had big breasts which trembled as she stamped her feet to keep warm. Unexpectedly, she put her tongue out and then whirled back to join the group. Their giggles erupted afresh.

'What's her name?' I asked.

'Sadie Bryant,' said Doss. 'She fancies herself.'

'I can see that.'

'It's when they start growing tits. They think it makes them special.' He bent down and made a snowball.

'You dare!' shrieked Sadie Bryant.

'Are you daring me then?' Doss moulded the snowball between his hands and drew back his arm. All the girls except Sadie Bryant ran away.

'You don't scare me,' she said. 'You or your friend.'

'You want to watch it,' said Doss.

'Look who's talking.'

I scooped up a handful of snow and threw it without thinking. It hit her in the face and some of it remained there, clogging her eyebrows and wetting her hairline. She brushed the snow away and again I saw her breasts shake beneath the blue swell of her raincoat. I stooped to gather more snow, but as I did so I was aware that a hush had fallen over the playground. I saw Doss's arm fall by his side and the snowball drop to the ground.

'Is this what they teach you at public school?' enquired a voice behind me. 'How to throw snowballs at girls. Very helpful, I'm sure.'

I turned to see Mr Buller smiling grimly at us both. Without warning he reached out and grabbed each of us by the ear. 'Report to me at morning break,' he said, emphasising each word with a jerk of the wrist. 'And in the meantime make your apology.' He let us go and beckoned to Sadie Bryant. 'Come here, girl. They want to say they're sorry.'

'Sorry,' I mumbled, feeling my ear turn to fire.

'Sorry,' said Doss.

'You see,' said Mr Buller. 'They're not complete savages. All one has to do is reinforce the lesson.'

He wagged his forefinger under my nose. 'Morning break. Don't forget.'

The main body of the school was like a sandwich loaf sliced up by partitions which were drawn across the hall as soon as the classes had assembled. The partitions did not exclude sound and the buzz, complaint and expostulation arising from three separate lessons rose and mingled like steam in the hull of the roof. I was in the class taken by Mr Buller. The subject was English Literature and Mr Buller read aloud from a book of short stories which we were then told to recapitulate and criticise. The story under review was 'The Tramp and the Organ', by O. Henry, a writer, said Mr Buller, who Understood Life.

'He knew the switchback of fortune,' said Mr Buller, spelling out his judgement at dictation speed so that we could copy it into our exercise books. Mr Buller gave out verdicts like badges which, if we wished to please him by reminding him of his sagacity, we were advised to pin to the lapel of the author for easy reference. O. Henry was Compassionate and told his stories with a Twist in the Tail. Lord Tennyson was Wise. John Masefield was a Master of the Common Tongue. He did not attempt a detailed analysis of their work, but provided a gloss to float us over the shallows of debate or through the most rudimentary of examination papers. Mr Buller believed in convenience. He was in favour of zip fasteners, instant soups and Esperanto. It was a language, he told us, which dissolved frontiers. If we had adopted it sooner, the present war would not have occurred. 'But now we are in it,' said Mr Buller, his pink parting aimed at us like an arrow, 'we should understand how it is being fought.'

The wall behind his desk was covered by campaign maps. Coloured pins marked emplacements, pushes and counter-offensives and thousands of miles of forests, lowlands and mountain ranges were pegged out like an obstacle course with lengths of twine which zigzagged wildly across the terrain. Months before Russia was invaded by Germany in the summer of 1941, Mr Buller knew that she was Coming In on Our Side. He produced a biography of Marshal Voroshilov by Dennis Wheatley entitled *Red Eagle* and urged us to read it as part of his programme of Knowing Our Allies.

His style of teaching was brisk and aphoristic. He allowed no time for reflection. For him the truth was self-evident and there to be acted upon. If he had worn a badge it would have been lettered Dynamic. As I discovered subsequently his philosophy also extended to the sports field. He tended to arrive at the pitch just as we were leaving, having spent the previous hour and a half in a bruising knockabout game. What we were most looking forward to was to scrape off the mud and (rarest of luxuries) to have a hot bath. Mr Buller's presence put paid to any such plan. He was there to take exercise and demonstrate how fit he was for a man of his age. We were the token opposition to his brilliant strategy, objects to be swept aside by his irresistible force.

Invariably he played centre forward, a position he felt entitled him to sole possession of the ball. If it was denied him he pounded alongside his team mate bellowing 'Pass!'

until, whatever the state of play, the ball was surrendered. He would then treat us to a display of dribbling, sprinting up and down the field, challenging each defender with a roar of 'Tackle me!' and sending each of them flat on his back until finally the goal mouth was clear and he could no longer delay punting the ball through the sagging posts.

If he was robbed of the ball by some intrepid back his cry of 'Foul!' was instant and automatic. As the evening dew descended, beading our hair and jerseys, he would stand arguing the justice of his case with the referee. He did not like to win too easily. The argument was an important part of the game. For one thing, it demonstrated democracy in action. For another, to protract the argument was to sweeten his final victory. Not only was justice done; it was seen to be done.

When bells rang to signal the mid-morning break Doss and I stood waiting in front of Mr Buller's desk. For several minutes he affected not to notice us. His head was bent and I saw his scalp glowing like ham the length of his parting. Then he looked up and nodded as though reminding himself of the business in hand. 'Throwing snowballs,' he said. 'A stupid practice.'

He glanced through the window at the grey sky across which clouds raced like bales of loose netting. 'How would they deal with this at your last school?' he demanded.

I shook my head. 'I don't know, sir.'

'A caning perhaps?'

'Perhaps.'

'Most likely, I should think. But we've learned better. Here we believe in making the punishment fit the crime.' He put his fingertips together as if applauding his own astuteness. 'You threw snow about,' he said. 'You shall clear it up. Ask Mr King to lend you a shovel apiece and make a path the length of the school playground. From entrance to exit. Not a track. A proper path. At least three feet wide.'

'When shall we do that, sir? asked Doss.

'As soon as you've had lunch. Before the first period this afternoon.'

'It'll most likely be snowing by then,' said Doss.

Mr Buller inclined his head. 'Very likely! But there'll be less underfoot if you do the job properly.' He laid his hands flat on the desk. 'Right you are then. Off you go.'

As Doss forecast, snow began to fall as we were digging the path. By the late afternoon our excavation looked like a shallow trench and the following day it was completely filled in. 'What a waste of time,' I said.

Doss tapped his fingertips together. 'Less underfoot though. Buller knows it and we know it. Doesn't it make you feel grand!'

On Saturday morning we accompanied Mr King to the Shop. It was in a basement beneath one of the girls' houses. Wooden benches lined the walls and in one corner there was a mountain of kindling which two boys were already parcelling in to small bundles. Chopping firewood for every house in the branch was, I discovered, a job which recruits to the Shop performed when bad weather kept them indoors. There were cleavers and small axes on the benches and a grindstone in the middle of the floor. Each piece of kindling had to conform to proportions ordained by Mr King. 'Get them the right size,' he told us. 'If it's too thick, it won't catch. If it's too thin, it's gone in a flash. What you want is a nice standard stick half an inch square, give or take a sliver. Keep your choppers sharp, go with the grain and it's as easy as pie.' He showed us how to set about it, halving, quartering and systematically reducing a block of pine into segments as pink as tinned salmon.

Doss and I began work, but Mr King took the axes from our hands. 'I've got another job for you two,' he said.

There was a heap of coke to be shovelled into the furnace room beneath the bakehouse. The ground on which it had been dumped was uneven and it was difficult to drive our shovels between the coke and the broken tarmac. After five minutes my hands were blistered and each time I lunged at the coke I hit a fang of stone so that the blade of my shovel chimed like a bell.

'Go below,' said Doss. 'I'll shove it down and you chuck it back to the far wall.'

I did as I was told, sliding down the chute in a rush of coke that tinkled on to the unseen flags below. The light bulb had fused, but there was the stub of a candle wedged into an empty Tizer bottle. I lit the candle and looked about me. The furnace roared behind its steel porthole. The whitewashed walls were swagged with cobwebs. There was a sweet smell of baking and as I found a ledge for the candle safely away from the fall of coke I noticed that the ceiling was shiny as if it had been freshly daubed with tar. I raised the candle to see better and as the flame touched the ceiling it split like cellophane. The gloss dissolved and hundreds of cockroaches rained down on my head.

I dropped the candle and in the rush of darkness I felt the insects scurry over my hands and face. I tripped over my shovel and the sharp edge cut into my knee. I tried frantically to climb the mountain of coke, but every step started a landslide which became an avalanche. It was like a dream in which, however hard I ran, I remained rooted to the spot, staked out for some awful beast. I heard myself sobbing. I could tast dust and the blood from my bitten lip. My knuckles were raw and there was grit in my eyes. Exhaustion claimed me. I gave up and, as I lay still, the horror receded.

I saw Doss's head framed by the mouth of the chute. 'What are you doing down there?' he demanded. 'Are you getting it shifted?'

I drew a deep breath and blew my nose. There was no sense in confessing how scared I had been. 'Less haste, more speed,' I said. It was a saying of my mother's and repeating it had always given me a feeling of reassurance, as if someone had squeezed my hand in passing. Now it made no sense. The talisman had lost its power.

I retrieved my shovel and dug it into the coke. Without looking, I aimed for the far wall and heard the cinders cascade to the floor. I did not relight the candle. There was nothing I needed to see. I already knew what lived in the darkness.

Three

Late that March a light aircraft which was carrying mail from Manchester crashed on the moors. The pilot was killed and a trail of letters which burst from one of the sacks pointed like a flare path to where the plane lay half-buried in a bog. One of the farm horses named Captain was sent to haul it out, but the salvage team returned on foot. Captain had sunk in the bog, still tethered to the plane, and after hours of trying to rescue him, the local vet was summoned.

'We had to shoot him,' Mr King told us. 'It was the kindest thing.' He blew his nose loudly and polished it with his handkerchief.

The story horrified us. Captain had been everyone's favourite. The previous summer, Ray recalled, he had ridden him bareback from the hayfield to the stables. 'He was a good old boy,' he said, 'good as gold.' We stared up at the moors as if confronting an enemy. No one lived up there. The water board had bought up all the farms for miles around to conserve the land as a watershed. Except for small flocks of sheep which it had proved impossible to round up, there were no animals to pollute the reservoir in the valley below. Five miles east towards Bury there was a deserted village in which one man remained to look after the churchyard. There was a quarry in which the red limbs of abandoned machinery poked through the water which had flooded it. And from north to south a shallow beck know as the Blood Stream sawed a channel through banks of heather and bilberry. Deposits of iron ore tarnished its bed, but local legend insisted that the colour came from the rusted armour of knights who had died fighting in the Wars of the Roses.

Those distant battles frequently seemed closer and easier to understand than the conflict which Mr Buller assured us now convulsed the world. His bulletins on the progress of the war, who was fighting whom and where, the number of casualties and the tally of tanks and planes destroyed were like chapters in a novel which became more fantastic day by day. In a sense, it was Mr Buller's war. We saw no newspapers and only rarely were we allowed to listen to the radio. Mr Buller told us what was happening; more than that, he interpreted events and described personalities so enthusiastically that they seemed to be his own creation.

Apart from the bus which arrived and departed three times a day we had no contact with life lived outside the Homes. On Sundays we marched down to the chapel in the village for morning and evening service. But we sat upstairs and the girls occupied reserved rows of pews below us. We did not speak to the villagers and they did not speak to us. Neither side made any overture of friendship. They tolerated us and we envied them. Sometimes a visiting preacher, unaware of the uneasy truce, would address us as fellow worshippers, equal members of the same congregation. But we all knew better. The preacher would depart and our relationship remained the same.

To the west of the Homes the land fell away into wooded folds and valleys. From my bedroom window I could see the railway line that ran southwards to Bolton, then Manchester and then the Potteries where my mother lived, ignorant of the fact that my letters to her were read and in effect censored by Mrs King who advised against imparting news which she considered in any way alarming. A mile away the line crossed a viaduct and on clear days we would watch the train scuttle over the slender arches, its head muffled in steam, its wheels beating a tattoo which we began to hear only after the last coach had disappeared from view.

I seemed to detect a difference in the rhythm of the

wheels according to the direction in which the train was headed. Going south the beat was jazzy. I was reminded of dance musice heard at home, a comic in my lap and a box of Liquorice Allsorts at my elbow. Northbound the tempo was more strict. I remembered the guard at Manchester urging me aboard the Northern Flier and the misery of that day would return, aching and unabated.

Although when I wrote to my mother I was careful to emphasise the positive aspects of life at the Homes – the number of goals scored, my position in class, my chances of attending a grammar school – my cheerfulness was largely assumed. I could not forget the zeal with which my mother and my uncle had offered evidence of my bad character to my last headmaster, or the haste with which they had dispatched me to the Homes. After two such betrayals, for that was how I regarded them, I decided it was wiser to dissemble than to confess. Telling tales was a risky business. It imposed a strain on the loyalty of others and my own credibility and, all in all, it was safer to remain silent.

There were also risks in forming friendships, so, instead, I sought allies. There was less of a commitment, less pain if the attachment did not endure. It was possible, I discovered, to be amiable, supportive, and keen within limits which were not defined, but understood. My relationship with Ray was based on our Potteries background and the possibility that, like him, I would attend a school outside the Homes. I relied on Doss to brief me on branch customs and taboos; how to press an advantage and how to avoid a confrontation. Skelly and Spiff were scroungers – one in the stores the other in the bakery – who supplemented rations and provided extras. We were mutually dependent. If we lied to each other, we expected our lies to be believed. If we expressed ambitions, we looked for sympathy. If we laid plots, we counted on support.

We owned few possessions. The week before I left for Lancashire my mother sent me with Mary, our housekeeper, to buy a new outfit. I chose the grey flannels which Spiff had forecast – incorrectly, as it turned out – would be confiscated, a green sports jacket with leather buttons and a blue double-breasted raincoat. I was better dressed than the rest of the boys, but my good luck was not resented. Eventually it would be someone else's turn. Only rarely did one boy steal from another; there was so little to covet. But the possessions of those who supervised us were fair game. They had power, they were privileged. If they could be plundered without anyone finding out, it was the thing to do.

At Mosscrop House the boys slept in three small dormitories, Sister Aggie's room was at the far end of the landing and Mr and Mrs King's bedroom was at the top of the stairs. One Wednesday afternoon – Mr King's half-day off when he and his wife had gone to see a film in Bolton – I met Skelly and Spiff dodging out of the Kings' bedroom. Skelly put his finger to his lips. 'Where's Aggie?' he hissed.

'In the kitchen.'

'What's she doing?'

'Seeing the kids don't smash anything washing up.' It was a job which could take from ten to twenty minutes, depending on how cag-handed the washers-up were. Sometimes, if they were particularly clumsy, the kitchen floor shimmered with broken crockery. Seeing the plates through the washing-up bowl, into the drying rack and stowed safely away into the cupboard was an ordeal for which Sister Aggie was peculiarly unsuited. Sudden noises made her jump. She expected the worst to happen and frequently it did. Her complexion became mottled. Her spectacles steamed over. She suspected that everyone was in league against her. Sometimes she cried. It was torture for her to watch a small boy stack a pile of plates in the sink, scour them with a dish-rag and then toss them one by one to the dryer standing by his side. If they let one slip it was conceivably an accident. If two were broken it might pass as a coincidence. Three breakages spelled a conspiracy. 'She'll be ages yet,' I said. 'What are you doing in there?'

Skelly crooked his finger. 'Come and see.'

It was a large, airy room with a Paisley counterpane on the bed and a chamber-pot beneath it. There was a small couch, a chest of drawers, a dressing table and a wardrobe with a mirrored front. Spiff turned the key and our reflected faces slid away as the door swung open. He reached inside and took out a black silk purse. It had a draw-string at the neck and Spiff plucked it loose. He shook the purse over the bed and dozens of pound notes fluttered on to the counterpane.

'How much is there?' I asked.

Skelly shook his head. 'We haven't counted.' He stirred the notes so that they spread into a grubby fan. 'Hundreds,' he said. 'Three hundred at least.'

'More,' said Spiff.

We stood admiring the riches on view. 'Have you taken any?' I asked.

'Not yet,' said Skelly.

'Are you going to?'

He nodded slowly. 'Just a couple of quid. They won't miss it.'

'Me too,' said Spiff. He extracted two notes from the centre of the fan and waved them under my nose. 'How about you?'

'I don't know,' I said.

'Are you scared?'

'Course not.'

'Go on then.' He stepped back and indicated the money. 'Be my guest.'

I took one note and stuffed it in my pocket. My heart was bouncing against my ribs and I swallowed noisily. 'Put the rest of it back and let's get out,' I said.

Spiff winked at Skelly. 'I told you he was scared.'

'It's Aggie,' I said. 'She'll be up here soon.'

Spiff opened the bedroom door and glanced down the stairs. From below us there came the crash of breaking china. 'Not for a while,' he said.

Skelly shovelled the money back into the bag and replaced it in the wardrobe. 'All right now?'

'Let's get out,' I said.

We crept on to the landing and closed the door behind us. Sister Aggie was at the foot of the stairs but she was not looking in our direction. She had a broken plate in one hand and was cuffing a small ginger-haired boy with the other. 'Don't hang about,' said Spiff quietly. He careered down the stairs and we followed, barging past Sister Aggie and racing through the dining room and into the yard.

'I'll be late for school if I don't hurry,' I said.

Skelly gripped my arm. 'Watch what you do with that money. Don't flash it around.'

'What are you going to do with yours?'

'Put it somewhere safe,' said Skelly.

'Till we can spend it,' said Spiff. 'Just find a hidey-hole. Away from the house.'

Where to dispose of the money was a problem. The village was out of bounds and, in any case, for a boy from the Homes to present a pound note at a village shop was to invite trouble. Homes boys had a reputation as thieves. A pound was a vast sum for any one of us to own and questions would most certainly be asked if we were rash enough to try and spend it where we could be identified. One possibility was to commission a boy such as Ray who went to school outside the branch to buy something in a more distant town. But Skelly advised against this. 'He doesn't like nicking,' he explained. 'He'd tell you to put it back.'

'Any road,' said Spiff, 'he'd say anything right now. He's in love.'

It was true. Everyone knew that Ray Clutton was in love with Gladys Fisher. She was fifteen, a year older than Ray, and she worked as a secretary in the branch administration office. She had blue eyes, a froth of fair curls and a full, flouncing figure. Every morning she came to work early so that she and Ray could meet in the office while he waited for his bus to school. They held hands and kissed several times, Ray told us, he had succeeded in unbuttoning her blouse and feeling her breast.

'Bare flesh?' demanded Doss.

'Certainly,' said Ray.

'Does she wear a bra?'

'Course she does.'

'Did you get inside it?'

Ray hesitated. 'Just about.'

'You never.'

'I was going to but the bus came.'

I listened enviously. Sadie Bryant was in the same house as Gladys Fisher and our relationship had progressed from throwing snowballs to exchanging notes in class and brushing against each other in the cloakroom as we queued for mid-morning milk. It was an experience which excited me more than I had thought possible. Sadie had short-sighted green eyes and to see me clearly without her glasses she tilted her head backwards so that she surveyed me down the length of her nose. It gave her a look of mystery and hauteur as if she was somehow unaware of the ripe body which swelled beneath her sweaters and gym slips, rippling as she walked and rocking like junket when she raised her hand to answer a question. She had a high, squeaky voice which I thought refined and when she laughed it was like the whinnying of a horse.

I was intensely curious about Sadie and all other girls. They seemed to belong to a different species and like an explorer I longed to make contact and know them better. My interest was almost scientific, but not quite. I genuinely sought knowledge, but I was far from detached. I yearned for involvement and intrigue. Outside school there were few opportunities to meet girls and to see them in private was always difficult. But the problems were themselves an incentive. Solving them was proof of passion. True love invariably found a way. It was an article of faith which, although it was never spelled out, we believed implicitly.

Because I was at the branch all day and saw Sadie at school, Ray relied on me to pass messages and arrange meetings between him and Gladys. 'Fix it so you can see your lass too,' he advised. 'We can go together. It means one of us can keep a lookout.' He drew a comb from his breast pocket and ran it through his hair. It was chestnut-coloured and bright with oil and Ray spent minutes at a time building up his quiff, pinching it between his fingers and the back of the comb so that it reared over his right eyebrow in a glossy pompadour. He was an expert on all hair dressings and would passionately debate the rival merits of Brylcreem, and Julysia. He saved the money given to him for tram fares in Bury and by walking to school whenever time allowed he was able to pay to have his hair cut by a barber of his choice.

At the branch our hair was cut once a month by Mr King or Mr Dunton, the other Labour Master. They aimed for a regulation crop which bared the neck and temples and left a ragged thatch too short to hold a proper parting. Prestige was measured by the inches you could preserve and Ray was the image of what we aspired to be. Not only his hair was immaculate. His skin glowed, he had no pimples or blackheads, he manicured his nails with a pair of folding scissors and his teeth were unchipped and brilliantly white. Morning and evening he scoured them with tooth powder and then faced the bathroom mirror, grinning at his reflection while the rest of us waited our turn.

'What did Gladys say?' he demanded. 'Can she come out tonight?'

'She said she'd try. Eight o'clockish.'

'Where?'

'The cloakroom. She daren't leave the house.'

Ray polished a favourite tooth with his index finger. 'Keeping an eye on her, are they?'

'That's what she says.'

'I shouldn't wonder. They know she's my lass.' he grinned at the mirror and his teeth blazed back.

The cloakroom of the girls' house was not an ideal place for an assignation, but there was no alternative. Sister Marion, the house mother, had a suspicious nature and she was in the habit of making spot checks throughout the evening to make sure that all her charges were indoors. During the day it was easier to arrange a meeting. At lunchtime it was reasonably safe to meet in the timber store behind the office block or in a side room of the laundry, lying squat beneath its flag of steam. We met in a reek of turpentine or among clean sheets, stacked like boulders, our comings and goings unnoticed in the traffic of the branch. But scrutiny intensified as the day wore on and in the evenings there had to be a good reason for anyone, especially a girl, to leave the house.

'They're leaving the back door open,' I said. 'We've got to go quietly.'

'What about the light?'

'Sadie's got a dud bulb. She'll change it over before we get there.'

'Clever lass,' said Ray. He gave his quiff a final squeeze and straightened his tie. 'Are you set, then?'

We put on our raincoats and climbed over the back wall of the yard. It had rained all day and the moon was hidden by banks of dark cloud. A dog barked at a farm three miles up the road but there was no other sound except for the wind soughing through the telegraph wires. On either side lamplight glowed through curtained windows, but the houses themselves were sealed against the night. I felt like a spy or a commando about to embark on a raid. Ray squeezed my arm. 'We'd be best off the road,' he said. 'We can cut across the meadow.'

'And get our feet soaked?'

I sensed although I could not see his grin. 'It's worth a wetting.'

The girls lived in Argyle House, the last outpost of the branch before the road dipped down towards the village. We could reach it by cutting behind the farm and the governor's house, jumping a stream and picking our way through a small plantation. By day it was an exposed route, but at night there was no one to observe us. We scrambled over the wall and into the field. I took a step forward and felt my foot sink into a cow pat.

'Just wipe it off,' said Ray.

'It's gone in my shoe.'

'Then watch where you're going.'

Our eyes were growing accustomed to the dark. I could distinguish tussocks of grass and a patch of blackberry bushes, humped like a whale. I avoided further cow pats and managed to jump the stream without falling in. We entered the plantation and Ray put up his hand. 'Hang on a second.'

A cyclist passed us, the light from his lamp dawdling over the wet tarmac. Abruptly it disappeared, cancelled by a bend in the road, and we went on, over the wall and up the drive of Argyle House. There was a smell of drains as we turned the corner. I put my hand to the back door and it swung open. There was a suppressed giggle from inside and someone took my hand. 'Don't make a sound,' said Sadie. Ray followed me through the door and closed it behind him. 'Over here,' said Gladys, 'behind the coats.'

Sadie tugged at my hand and I went where I was taken. She pulled me into a corner behind the hanging coats and draped them in front of us like a curtain. Our legs were still visible, but I knew that there was a dead bulb in the light socket. We were safe, I thought; no one could see us. Distantly I heard a piano being played. There were occasional bursts of laughter, like water gushing from a pump. I turned to face Sadie and out noses collided. The strap of a satchel grazed my neck and when I breathed in I seemed to be inhaling gabardine.

'Kiss me,' said Sadie.

'Kiss her,' said Ray bossily.

He and Gladys were in the opposite corner. In a seepage of light from the hall door I could see their knees and the toe-caps of Ray's shoes, shockingly obvious in the long line of wellington boots. I felt a pang of anxiety which I tried to allay by bearing down on Sadie's open mouth.

She flinched and pulled away. 'Sorry,' I said.

'You made me bite my lip.'

'Practice makes perfect,' said Ray.

'Mind your own business,' I hissed.

It was worrying to have bungled a kiss, but the shoes worried me more. If I could see them, then so could anyone else who looked in the right direction. I was about to whisper a warning when the hall door swung open and a hand reached in for the light switch. 'Blessed thing!' Sister Marion exclaimed when the light failed to go on. She peered into the cloakroom, reaching out with one hand as if to shred the unwanted darkness. 'Are you girls there?' she demanded. 'You can't hide from me. I know you're there.'

We pressed back into the corner trying desperately to breathe without making a sound. Through a gap in the coats I saw Ray inch back his feet, one after the other. His shoes grated faintly on the floor and Sister Marion turned towards him.

'Who's there?' Her voice was uncertain as if she hoped that she had misheard. 'If anyone's there come out this instant.'

We still did not move and she retreated to the hall. 'I'm going to get my torch,' she threatened. 'Then we'll see what's what.'

Her footsteps receded. We heard a door open and close and as if an order had been flashed on a screen for us to obey, Ray and I burst through the coats with the girls close behind us. 'We'd best be off,' said Ray. He prodded me in the ribs. 'Kiss her goodnight then.'

Sadie's tongue brushed my lips and I jerked away as if I had licked a live wire. She hooked an arm round my neck and pulled me back. I felt her mouth pulpy beneath mine and maintained the contact for a count of five. There should be more to it, I thought. My instinct was to melt into her, to flow like hot fudge in a saucepan, filling every indentation and cranny. But my lips remained rigid. My body was braced like a goalie ready to make a save. My neck ached with the strain.

Sadie let me go and opened the door. 'See you tomorrow,' she said. I dodged outside and waited in the dark while Ray completed his farewell. He liked to pretend that although delay was dangerous, he was so drunk with love that he could not bear to break away. He kept releasing Gladys, making a half-turn and then returning to pounce on her upturned face like a cat snapping up the last morsels in its dinner dish.

We heard footsteps in the corridor and she thrust him into the yard. 'Run,' she said. 'Sister's coming.'

We sprinted down the path, across the road and into the plantation. Round the corner of Argyle House we saw the bright eye of a torch blinking after us and heard Sister Marion's shrill halloo. What she was shouting was indistinguishable, but her voice was high and angry. Like the yelping of a horn it pursued us over the stream and half-way across the meadow.

I grabbed Ray's arm. 'Hold on a sec. I'm out of breath.'

We stopped in the middle of the dark field and listened. No one was coming after us. A breeze passed lightly over my face and looking up I saw that the clouds had parted and the stars shone through. A train crossed the viaduct and we saw the spark of its fire, followed as always by the remote racket of its wheels.

'Are you fit?' asked Ray.

'Just about.'

'You need to cut down on the fags,' he said. 'You shouldn't be out of puff as soon as that.'

I shook my head. 'It's not smoking.'

'What is it then?'

'Nerves,' I said.

He grinned and I saw his teeth flash in the starlight. 'Nerves are what posh people have. I was right first time about you.'

I did not tell Ray about the money I had stolen from Mr King's bedroom. I folded the pound note between the pages of a letter from my mother and kept it in my wallet. No one was likely to look for it there, I thought. Nor was there any indication that Mr King was aware that he had been robbed.

'There'll be a chance to spend it soon,' said Skelly. 'It's the Good Friday walk next month.'

The walk was a tradition of the Homes, eagerly discussed by all, but dreaded by some as the day approached. I was baffled by their apprehension. 'What's so dreadful about a walk?' I asked.

'It's not just a little stroll,' said Doss. 'It's a bloody long trek and you have to keep up.'

'How far?'

'Twenty miles or so. Depending on how strong their legs are.'

'Whose legs?'

'Whoever's taking us. King if he's told to. Buller if he wants to show us how brave he is. Last year he had a car pick him up half-way. Said he had to get back to see someone.' Doss laughed disbelievingly. 'Wanted to soak his blisters more like.'

'Where do we go?'

He made a wide sweep with his arm. 'There and back. Over the moors to Peel's Monument, then all the way home. It's none so bad if it's fine, but usually it's pissing down.'

We looked up at the moors where Captain lay dead and buried in a peat bog. There were huge glacial rocks where the bracken had peeled away and gulleys in which you could lie completely protected while the wind screamed overhead. Birds nested there: curlew and snipe and buntings which flitted between the barbed arms of the gorse. In the summer it would be a different country, honeyed with the scent of heather. But in the early spring it looked sodden and hostile; a shelf over which the weather poured without interruption.

'Do the lasses go too?'

'Don't be daft,' said Doss. 'They're not tough enough.'

'I see.' The walk, I realised, was an initiation ceremony. If you completed the circuit – complaining perhaps, but showing fortitude – you passed muster. If you dropped out, you could expect twelve months' teasing. 'I've always cared for a nice promenade,' I said.

'Promawhat?'

'Promenade. Taking the air. Going for a constitutional.' I did not feel as cocky as I sounded, but I thought jauntiness was called for.

Doss looked me up an down. 'Tell me what you care for when you've done it,' he said.

I remembered his warning at nine o'clock on Good Friday when we assembled in the school playground, winking and waving at several of the older girls who were there to see us off. Mr King wore his second-best brown trilby and had his walking stick tucked under his arm like a baton. There was no sign of Mr Buller but as we were about to leave he came trotting into the yard, a haversack on his back. We each carried a picnic lunch – one corned beef sandwich, one jam sandwich, a rock cake, a hot cross bun and an apple – wrapped in a sheet of greaseproof paper. From the stores Skelly had scrounged a large bottle of cream soda. It was hidden in a shoulder bag and if we wanted to share it, said Skelly, we had to take turns in carrying it.

'Right you are then,' bawled Mr King. 'Form fours!'

It was the marching order we adopted when we attended service in the village chapel. Good soldiers never look sloppy, Mr King told us. We were expected to make a good impression. People remarked on whether or not we looked smart and our turn-out reflected on him. 'Small boys to the front, bigger boys to the rear,' he ordered. As he had previously explained, our pace was determined by the slowest walker. We took our places, arguing over seniority until Mr King plucked a whistle from his waistcoat pocket and blew a prolonged blast. 'If there's any more messing about you won't go,' he threatened. 'There's plenty of jobs need doing about the place. It's entirely up to you.' The hubbub lessened and we stood waiting. 'Atten-*shun!*' roared Mr King. 'Left turn. By the left, quick march!'

The girls cheered and we headed up the hill towards the

moors. Mr Buller led the way, swinging his arms and glancing over his shoulder at the column that straggled behind him. 'Can't we go any faster?' he demanded.

'It's the little lads,' said Mr King soothingly. 'They can't keep up.'

Mr Buller snorted as if he had a crumb stuck in his throat. 'If they can't keep up, they won't grow up.' He stood by the side of the road and marked time. 'Left, right. Left, right,' he chanted. stepping up the pace and throwing us into complete disorder. 'Hopeless,' he said as the column shambled past him. 'Tell them they can break ranks. There's no one to see them now.'

Mr King blew his whistle and gave the order. 'No straggling,' he warned, 'and no smoking in the rear. Just remember I've got eyes in the back of my head.'

Skelly cupped his cigarette in his hand and expelled a thin stream of smoke which dissolved instantly in the haze of breath and mist which hung over us. 'Keep looking,' he murmured. He was not noted for his courage, but he had an insolence which drove him to take risks.

'You'll get copped one of these days,' said Ray.

Skelly drew hard on the concealed cigarette. 'Not by him I won't.'

When we reached the top of the hill rain began to fall. For five minutes it drizzled and then the heavens opened. I envisaged a huge bag filled with water and slung between clouds which someone had attacked with a garden fork. The rain fell in perpendicular lines, and kept on falling as if holes had been punched in the sky itself and the wounds would never heal. The surface of the road hissed and bubbled. Streams filled the ditches. The new bracken was spangled with brilliants which melted and reformed again and again.

I turned up the collar of my raincoat, but it was too late. My shirt was already soaked. The turnups of my trousers were heavy and I could feel the cold seeping through the worn soles of my shoes. 'We've not gone far. We could turn back,' I said.

Doss raised an eyebrow, 'What happened to the promenade?'

'Bugger the promenade.'

'I could do with a promenade right now,' said Spiff. 'Beside the seaside, beside the sea.'

'Not that sort of promenade,' said Doss. 'Get him to tell you.'

I would not respond. We plodded on and after a while the rain stopped. 'How about a song,' shouted Mr Buller. 'Everybody sing.' He climbed on to a wall and as we filed past he struck up 'She'll Be Coming Round the Mountain'. A few thin voices joined him from the head of the column, but the chorus fell flat. 'Come on, you big boys,' he called, 'let's hear from you.'

We opened and closed our mouths without uttering a sound and he watched us suspiciously. 'You there,' he said pointing to Skelly. 'You're not singing.'

'Sore throat, sir.'

'You then,' said Mr Buller, aiming his finger at Doss.

'Voice breaking, sir.'

Mr Buller walked alongside us, his rain-soaked haversack oozing water. 'I can't imagine why you want to come on a walk like this,' he said. 'You have no community spirit. None at all. Here we are, Mr King and myself, giving up our free time. And what happens? Are you grateful? No you are not. You are a disagreeable bunch of malcontents.' He put on a spurt and joined Mr King further up the road.

'What's a malcontent?' asked Skelly.

'Someone who likes a promenade,' said Doss. 'Walks are different.'

We stopped for lunch in the barn of an abandoned farm. A pair of magpies were building a nest in a hole in the wall and we watched them fly in and out carrying twigs and wisps of wool. 'You're to leave them be' said Mr Buller. 'I don't want any boy climbing up there and disturbing them.'

'Don't magpies kill fledglings, sir?' asked Doss. 'That's what we were told in nature study.'

Mr Buller bit down on a cold sausage and chewed energetically before replying. He swallowed hard and raised his finger. 'The weak perish and the strong survive. That's how the balance of nature is maintained.'

Skelly looked puzzled. 'But, sir,' he said. 'What if you've got fifty magpies and half a dozen larks. There's no balance there. And there'll be no larks before long.'

'Foolish boy,' said Mr Buller. 'There'll always be more than half a dozen larks.'

'But what if there weren't?' Skelly persisted.

'Hungry magpies,' said Doss.

By the end of the meal rain was falling once more. Peel's Monument was less than a mile away and as we set off again it was cheering to think that we had at least reached the half-way mark. The Monument was a granite tower with a spiral flight of steps inside it leading to an observation platform. It had been built, although no one could explain why, to commemorate the birth of Sir Robert Peel. In his memory we climbed the steps and stared dutifully out over acres of drenched moorland. Nothing stirred except the rain. We marched down the steps and Skelly produced the last of the cream soda. As we drank it we heard Mr Buller talking to Mr King.

'I shall have to phone my wife,' he said. 'I'd completely forgotton I'd asked Mr Parker to dinner. She won't be expecting him at all. I'm afraid I shall have to leave you on your own. Will you be able to manage?'

Mr King came to a modified form of attention. 'Perfectly, sir.'

'It quite slipped my memory,' Mr Buller went on. 'My wife will have to come and meet me. You say there's a phone box in the next village?'

'Just down the hill, sir.'

'Excellent. That's saved the day.' Mr Buller chafed his hands, his good humour restored by the prospect of an early release. 'I'd hate you to think I was deserting you,' he said. 'It's just that we have some vital business to discuss. I'm sure you understand.'

Mr King looked suitably grave. 'Certainly, sir.'

'Good man, good man. Now, which way do we go?'

Mr King pointed with his walking stick. He could have been a prophet indicating the promised land instead of a small moorland village, but our spirits rose. 'Don't spend more than a quid,' Skelly warned Spiff. 'We don't want them asking questions.'

Only the general store was open. There was a display of vegetables, a rack of soft drinks and a selection of bread and buns behind the counter. One flustered woman tried to cope with twenty orders at a time.

'Give us four balm cakes, missus,' called Skelly.

'And a bottle of Vimto,' added Doss.

Spiff gave her his best smile. 'Do you have any Player's Bachelor Tipped?' he asked.

She tried to peer over our heads. 'What are you boys doing back there? You keep your hands to yourselves.'

'Don't you fret,' said Skelly. 'I'll see they don't take anything.' He pocketed his change and put the bag of balm cakes to his nose. 'Smashing,' he said. 'Just don't you fret.'

Half an hour later and a mile away we examined our loot. Spiff had a tin of peaches, Skelly had a large onion and Doss had a packet of soap flakes. 'What about you?' he enquired.

I showed them a card of shoelaces which I had filched from a box beside the cash register. 'They're brown,' said Doss. 'Your shoes are black.'

'Better than your soap flakes.'

'I could sell them,' said Doss.

'Who to?'

'Anyone. Whoever buys Skelley's onion.'

Rain still fell intermittently. We made our way back to the Monument like an army of mercenaries, our duty done, our pillaging over. It was not important what we stole. What mattered was that by stealing we had achieved some sort of balance. The have-nots had defeated the haves. Bit by bit we discarded our booty. The soap flakes were tucked into the heart of a drystone wall. The onion was hurled at a flock of sheep. I decided I might be able to dye the laces with marking ink. We opened the tin of peaches with Skelly's clasp knife and ate them dripping and lucent, between our fingers.

Before we reached the Monument we saw Mrs Buller driving the governor's Jaguar towards us along the bottom road. Mr Buller stepped in front of the car with his hand raised. 'Time to part company,' he said blithely. 'Is there any boy who feels too tired to walk home? If so, he can come with me.' He stood like a salesman holding open the rear door of the car and the cosy smell of carpeting steeped in tobacco smoke wafted over us as the rain glued our wet coats to our shoulders.

No one moved and Mr King strutted backwards and forwards looking for volunteers. 'Anyone with sore feet? Anyone who wants a ride home?'

Mr Buller rattled the door handle and glanced at his watch. 'No takers then, Mr King?'

'Apparently not, sir.'

'They must suit themselves. I have to be off.' He slammed the door shut and slid into the front seat beside his wife. She switched on the ignition and the Jaguar rolled forward.

'Three cheers for the governor,' shouted Doss. He ran beside the car speeding it on its way and we cheered as it rounded the bend and accelerated down the hill. Mr Buller's window opened a few inches and his hand emerged, the fingers fluttering in farewell.

We watched the car drown in the mist. 'What was all that about?' demanded Mr King.

Doss smiled ingenuously. 'What was what about, sir?'

'Cheering and that.'

'Mark of respect, sir.'

Mr King tucked his stick more securely under his arm. 'You want to watch it,' he said. 'People can catch on, you know.'

The sun came out shortly after we passed the Monument and our coats began to steam as if we were wearing hot poultices under our shirt. Someone started to sing 'She'll Be

Coming Round the Mountain'. The chorus sweetened and swelled and when I looked over my shoulder I saw that Mr King was joining in.

Four

IT WAS Mr King's job, he claimed, to prepare us for Life. 'Never mind what they teach you at school,' he said. 'That's all well and good. It might come in handy, speaking a bit of French. And you should know how to do your sums. If two and two don't make four, you're in trouble. But Life's more than that. It's dealing with people. It's finding out how they tick. It's learning how to get the best out of things.'

On wet Saturday mornings when the view from the basement windows of the Shop was of rain-streaked roads and roofs like sealskin it required only a little guile to coax him into telling tales which illustrated what he meant. Most of them cast Mr King if not as a hero, then as a brilliant manipulator who was foxier and defter than his adversaries. When he was in India, he told us, he made a point of being the first customer of the day in the local bazaar. 'They had a superstition in those parts,' he said. 'They thought it was bad luck to turn down the first person who wanted to buy something. So you could go on beating them down. It didn't matter what you offered. They always said yes in the end.' If need be, he added, you could speed the negotiations by spitting on whatever you wanted. 'With your gob on it they wouldn't sell it to anyone else.'

'Why not?' asked Doss.

'Like I say, superstition. It's what they believe out there. Spitting on something makes it unclean. They just want to get shut of it.' Mr King loaded his pipe with cut plug, ramming it down with his index finger and squinting along the stem as he lowered the match to the bowl. His pipe rarely left his mouth. He took it with him into the bathroom. He took it to bed. During meals it lay like a pistol beside his plate. Visiting strange houses to move furniture or unblock sinks he always asked permission to smoke it and he was never refused. 'Women like the smell,' he explained. 'They think it's manly.'

He had a distinctly ambivalent attitude towards work. He was proud of being able to turn his hand to anything. He was the only man on the branch who could kick the farm tractor into life on a winter morning and he was an expert bricklayer and builder of walls. But he spent much of his time scheming how to avoid taking on a job. He suffered from a pathological idleness, an instinct to skive which packed his bones like marrow. He never acknowledged as much to us, but watching him screw his ingenuity to the shirking point was a lesson we effortlessly absorbed.

Sometimes he would invoke sciatica, sometimes a sprained back. Nursing his pipe he would recall his time in the army when the hours of duty were like bleached and busy anthills in green fields of leisure. He was a great believer in King's Regs, but if a detour could be discovered around the tasks of the day without an actual breach of rules he counted it a personal triumph. 'One thing I learned in the army was look busy,' he told us. 'Always look as if you're going somewhere. Don't hang about. Walk briskly.' He studied our expressions to gauge whether or not we were ready to receive his most valuable item of advice. 'Whenever possible,' he said, 'carry a piece of paper. No one's going to ask what it is. But it looks official. It works wonders.' He leaned back exhausted. It was as if he had handed on the torch and now counted on us to do likewise.

Working with Mr King we learned how to modulate our effort. He stressed the importance of making a job last. There was no point, he said, in going at it mad-hatted only to find ourselves at twelve-fifteen with the chore completed and another forty-five minutes to fill. He encouraged us to find a rhythm and stick to it. 'It's like boxing,' he said. 'You spend the first round getting to know each other. Then you get down to business, but you don't want to wrap it up too soon. There are people out there who've paid good money to see you. And you don't want to do yourself an injury.

Nor the other bloke. So you give them a demonstration. You do your best, but you don't kill youself. And it's the same with working. Do it nice and easy. Get the job done, but do it in your own good time.'

He would start us off on a job by making sure that we had the right tools and knew how to use them. He wanted no accidents on his record so that he took care to whom he issued axes or any other implement he considered dangerous. He had a knack for finding someone in the work detail who could be trusted; someone who subscribed to his own philosophy and could, in Mr Kings's words, turn his jib to the wind. But we were never left entirely to our own devices. 'Get on with it on your own,' he told us; 'just remember, I shall be Putting in an Appearance.' It was the only warning he gave and there was no appeal.

Muck-spreading in one of the top meadows one breezy morning I saw Mr King leaning on the gate a quarter of a mile away. On the far side of the field, two of the boys were larking about. One of them loaded his fork with dung and threw it at the other. The shot was returned and a battle began. Without haste Mr King climbed the gate and strolled across the meadow. He reached the two combatants before they knew he was there. 'Fun and games,' he said. 'Can I join in?' He grabbed their collars and banged their heads together, then booted them often and in turn until they stumbled to their knees. 'Don't lie there,' he advised them. 'I told you to get on with it.'

We were not afraid of Mr King. Living with him was like living with an ogre whose brawn was chiefly employed in frightening off others. He looked after his own and his reputation as a hard man extended even to those of us he was meant to discipline. He was not fair, but we did not expect equity. We looked for rules which, although they were harsh, were easy to understand. If we transgressed we did not automatically expect to be punished. There was always the chance of getting away with it. 'The worst crime', Mr King instructed us, 'is being found out.' He turned a blind eye to many of our offences, frequently because he could not be bothered to take the appropriate action, but also because he knew we were playing a game of some sort. He was unsure of its object, but instinctively he knew that sometimes we should be allowed to win. Stealing Mr King's money was an important move in the game which went beyond theft, beyond any concept of property. It meant that because we had not been found out we held an advantage. We were secret sharers. We had claimed our entitlement and we banked it against any outrage or injustice which might plague us in the future.

Mrs King was Mr King's cross. He treated her with a gallantry which would have been extreme even at a royal court – opening doors, lowering her into chairs, finding her place in her library book – but it all seemed a little theatrical. Mrs King was delicate while Mr King was rough. It was role-playing which they performed not only for their own satisfaction, but also as a means of manipulating the household. If Mr King threatened to thrash one of the boys, Mrs King would plead for mercy. If Mrs King had a headache the rule of silence was instant and absolute. Her sensibilities decreed what radio programmes we were allowed to listen to. Her concern that we would provoke Mr King by horseplay in the bedrooms would act as a bromide. They worked in tandem, each using the other's temperament as a threat or excuse for his or her own inclinations.

There was no doubt that Mrs King's health was poor. It was because she needed country air that Mr King had taken the job at the Homes. It was a comedown, he implied. His army career, while not distinguished, had been exemplary. And as a chauffeur his quarters, as he described them, had been luxurious. He had also been on intimate terms with his boss, an industrialist who rewarded his loyalty with lavish tips or gifts of cigars. 'And flowers,' said Mr King, his hands moulding the air into enormous bouquets. Every Friday the gardener would fetch Mrs King a basket of blooms so that she had flowers for the weekend. 'There's none of that here.'

He did not go so far as to blame Mrs King for the change in his fortunes, but he left us in no doubt that by putting her first he had wound up a poor second. Most of all he missed his chauffeur's uniform. 'Bottle green serge it was, with a stand-up collar and two rows of brass buttons, a peaked cap and breeches with piping down the sides.'

'And boots,' prompted Doss.

'Black boots,' said Mr King. 'Up to the knee and shiny like those they wear in the cavalry.' He sucked on his pipe and we mourned with him for his lost glory.

One day he told us that he and Mrs King were moving into new quarters. 'Doctor's advice,' he said. 'Mrs King's been doing too much. She's been told to put her feet up.' He had already spoken to Mr Buller, and they were taking over a farm-worker's cottage close to the school. 'She'll miss you,' he said, 'no doubt about that. But Mrs King comes first.' He assumed the fierce expression he habitually wore when describing the call of duty.

We were appalled by the news. The prospect of being abandoned by a couple whose authority, though formidable, could sometimes be subverted was upsetting. We were to become like everyone else. The tigers had all been tamed. The Sisters were taking over and it was with foreboding that we looked forward to a regiment of women.

As it turned out we were right to do so, but for reasons we did not expect. We had not imagined anyone as awful as Sister Beryl. We were used to irritation, abuse and the occasional cuff to amplify a point or check a misdemeanour. But we were not prepared for malice. Sister Beryl had not wanted to come to Mosscrop. She resented being there. She disliked and despised us and she made her feelings plain on the day she arrived. 'I've heard about Mosscrop boys,' she said. 'Dirty, deceitful little beasts who ought to be in Borstal. Well, I won't put up with it. Don't think for one second that because there's no man in the house you can get away with it. I've told Mr Buller and he's promised me that he'll deal with anyone who gives any trouble. He knows what I'm up against. He's on my side.'

We believed her. Mr Buller liked to be considered progressive. He spoke at headmasters' conferences. He was in demand as a lay preacher and took part in regional Brains Trusts as an authority on youth. He talked of reform and social change when the war had been won. But on all important issues he lacked nerve. He founded a debating society – a forum, he said, at which we could all speak our minds. But after the first session (the topic was Whether or not the branch could be run as a Democracy) he disbanded it for ever. 'I am not providing a platform for rudeness,' he declared. 'Courtesy is the first rule of debate and from start to finish that rule has been flouted.' We had brought personalities – including his own – into the argument and he was not prepared to put up with it. We were amused rather than sorry to see the society abolished but it was no more than we expected. Mr Buller did not want his views challenged, only endorsed. He did not like to feel the boat being rocked; it made him queasy. There was no doubt that he would back Sister Beryl. He did not dare to do otherwise.

She had come from one of the girls' houses where, we learned, she was known as Pod. It was easy to see why. She had a pink sulky face with a protruding lower lip which glistened with saliva. Her hair was the colour of old bracken and curiously dull, as if the oils had been baked out of it. Her shoulders drooped and her belly protruded like a giant tear-drop which only her dress prevented from rolling to the floor. She looked sullen, uncomfortable and pregnant; in pod, so to speak. I thought I had never heard a better nickname.

Her spectacles had gold frames and she wore a heavy gold ring on her right hand. As she spoke she pleated the back of her skirt between her fingers, crimping the blue silk to show several inches of pink slip. It was as vivid as a newly healed burn and just as shocking. I did not want to look, but the skirt kept rising and falling and I could not turn away. Sister Beryl intercepted my stare and let go of her skirt. 'Cheeky monkey,' she said. 'What d'you think you're looking at?'

I shook my head. 'Nothing.'

'Mosscrop ways,' said Sister Beryl. 'Dirty habits and dirty minds.'

She licked her bottom lip and it shone like a bathroom tile. 'You there,' she said to Spiff. 'What muck have you got on your hair?'

'Just Vaseline.'

'Vaseline, is it? Well, you can get that off for a start. Hair-washing tonight and everyone has a bath.'

'Friday night's bath night,' said Spiff.

Sister Beryl put her hands on her hips so that her belly stuck out even further. 'You'll bath when I say so.'

'Who's going to make me?'

'I'll make you,' said Sister Beryl. 'Me or Mr Buller. You can take your pick.'

Sister Aggie had moved out at the same time as the Kings and the new deputy was named Sister Anna. She was a big woman with a mass of sandy hair plaited and coiled at the nape of her neck. Her eyes were green and the contours of her face looked as though they had been planed off in quick positive strokes, leaving high cheekbones and a resolute jaw. It was evident that she and Sister Beryl did not get on. Sister Anna was no disciplinarian. She played cricket in the yard with the smaller boys, clouting the ball across the road and into the meadow behind the farm, piling on the runs, her entire body shuddering with effort as she pounded up and down the tarmac.

When she supervised bed-making we would sometimes throw a blanket over her head and tickle her while she was trying to tug it off until she lost her balance and fell backwards on the mattress where she lay panting, her eyes bright and her hair spilling on to the pillow. It was a dangerous game. It was exciting to see Sister Anna's plump legs jumping like trout in her black stockings and the temptation to touch her, to accidentally jog her breasts and experience the shock of that elastic flesh, was almost irresistible.

For her, I think, as well as us. She said she had brothers. They had been brought up together and the wrestling and rough-housing was a kind of body language with which she was familiar. The message, though, was confused. What began as innocent play could turn into something hot and heart-stopping and without warning we would find ourselves hanging face over face, thigh upon thigh, suddenly stilled by an awareness of the risk we were running. It did not always happen like that and the unpredictability was part of the attraction. We dared each other to take a chance, tumbling further and further towards an edge we knew was there until we would glimpse the gulf beneath us and fall back, shaking and out of breath.

There was no such intimacy with Sister Beryl. The aversion she felt towards us was wholly returned. I found it unpleasant to be in the same room with her. The cologne she wore, which would have been fragrant on another skin, seemed to mask a grosser smell, something rank and anxious which she could not disguise. It was like an aura, generated by her constant bad temper, which warned us off in unmistakable terms.

On the first bath night Sister Anna was detailed to take charge of the smaller boys. In pairs they were seen into the two baths and two showers while we waited our turn in the dining room. We watched them emerge, their faces flushed, their skin polished by soap. 'Nobody's watching me have a bath,' said Ray.

'Or me,' said Skelly.

Spiff showed us a new jar of Vaseline in his locker. 'I've only just got this. I'm not going to let it go to waste.' He ran a comb through his hair and wiped it on his sleeve. 'Brand new,' he said. 'There's enough there for months.'

Mr King had allowed us to take our baths without supervision. Unannounced, he had sometimes Put in an Appearance, to make sure that hot water was not being wasted or that the floor was not awash. But there was no sense of intrusion. Our privacy was not violated. With Sister Beryl we felt we were being spied on. Even when she was not actually present we were apprehensive. At any moment we expected to see her slumped figure in the doorway and hear her complaining voice. 'Let's get in there now,' said Ray. 'If we jam a chair under the latch she can't get the door open.'

'What if she fetches Buller?' asked Spiff.

'She can fetch him,' said Ray. 'She's not bloody well gawping at me.'

There was no doubt that he meant what he said. Gladys Fisher had made him promise not to swear (a demonstration of her power, rather than her prudery) and for Ray to use a word forbidden by her showed that he was unusually determined.

'How about this one?' said Doss. He pulled a chair from beneath the table and lifted it for us to see.

'It'll do. Are you coming?'

We followed Ray to the bathroom where Sister Anna was drying the hair of a boy named Bobby Cairns. His father was West Indian and he was the colour of an old penny, not black but a dull brown as though many hands had fondled the copper.

'Are you done?' asked Ray.

Sister Anna paused, her fingers busy in Bobby's curls. 'Almost.'

'Can you finish him off outside?'

'If you like.'

She steered Bobby into the washroom, still shrouded in the towel, and we filed past her, Doss clasping the chair to his chest. He shut the door and propped it beneath the latch. 'That ought to do it.'

Ray kicked a bath mat towards him. 'Stick that under its legs. We don't want it skidding all over the shop.' He fitted a plug into one of the baths and ran the water. 'Bags this one.'

We took off our clothes and piled them in the driest

corner. As I stepped under the shower I heard Sister Beryl come into the washroom. She spoke to Sister Anna and although the words were indistinct, her tone of voice – an aggrieved screech – warned us of her irritation. She pounded on the door and the chair shifted on the wet tiles. 'You boys come out of there.'

'We're having a bath,' shouted Ray. 'Like you told us to.'

'I didn't say go off and have it on your own. You can come out this instant.'

Ray did not reply but jerked two fingers at the door. He grinned at me and through the curtain of spray I saw his teeth flash. Lately he had taken to polishing them with a pad of dry flannel, buffing the enamel until each tooth appeared to be sheathed in a film of glass.

'Raymond Clutton, you're the senior boy,' called Sister Beryl. 'I hold you responsible. Do you hear what I say?'

Ray turned his taps full on and indicated to us to do the same. The pipes rattled, the water pattered down and Sister Beryl's voice was submerged. I opened my mouth and gargled. Spiff began to sing 'Onward Christian Soldiers' and Skelly and Doss joined in .

'Can't hear you, Sister,' shouted Ray. 'There's too much noise in here.'

We stayed behind our barricade for an hour. Then we dried ourselves and dressed, feeling clean and subdued and slightly nervous. Sister Beryl was waiting for us in the dining room. She stood with her back to the fire, her thumbs hooked into her belt and her belly bulging like a blue sandbag. 'Clever monkeys,' she said. 'Did you enjoy your bath?'

'Not bad,' said Spiff, more perkily than he felt.

'Did you wash that Vaseline off?'

'Yes, I did.'

'Just as well,' said Sister Beryl. 'You won't be getting any more hot water for a while. You've had your ration for the week.'

'Water's not rationed,' said Ray.

'Fuel is,' said Sister Beryl. 'You've used more than your

fair share this evening. So we have to make it up. Or rather, you do. Our bathroom upstairs has an immersion heater, which is handy because I propose letting the furnace out. And you boys can make do with cold water.'

I saw several strands of Spiff's hair spring up from his scalp and stand to attention. 'That's not fair,' he said. 'You can't get muck off with cold water.'

Sister Beryl folded her arms over her stomach so that it looked as if she was hugging a bolster. 'You should have thought of that.'

'We'll manage,' said Ray.

'You'll have to pass inspection,' said Sister Beryl. 'There'll be no tide marks and no dirty knees. You can make use of that scrubbing brush.'

Ray gave her his best smile. 'Right you are, Sister.'

The gleam of his perfect teeth unsettled her as he had intended. 'We all know how fussy you are Raymond Clutton,' she said. 'We'll just have to see how you get on.' She marched out of the room, but at the door she turned. 'And I don't want to find any of you dirty monkeys using our bathroom. It's out of bounds to you and don't you forget it.'

The door slammed shut and Ray turned his smile on us. It was like seeing the play of a searchlight – so confident, so powerful that I almost winced. 'Don't you fret,' he said. 'There'll be plenty of hot water when you want it.'

'Easy for you to say,' said Doss. 'You can wash at school.'

'And you lot can wash at the smithy,' said Ray. 'They've got tanks full of hot water there.'

He was right, of course. The smithy was our name for the engineering and electrical department where horses had once been shod, but which now dealt mainly with car repairs and lighting installations. The smithy apprentice was responsible for firing the boiler which heated the water for the branch laundry, and one of the tanks was fitted with a small brass tap from which one could fill teapots or baths, if necessary.

'All we need do is take our soap and towel over there,'

said Ray. 'There's no need to say anything to old Pod. Let her guess what's going on.'

And so for seven days we washed, morning and evening, at the smithy. It meant getting up half an hour earlier and returning home fifteen minutes later than usual. But our knuckles and necks showed no trace of grime when they were inspected by Sister Beryl and on the next bath night she remained in the washroom while we sluiced and showered ourselves next door. It was a small victory, but significant. The only one to sustain a significant loss of face was Spiff, whose stock of Vaseline was confiscated. Seeing him with his hair falling into his eyes, Mr Buller marched him to Mr Dunton who performed instant surgery. That night we studied his shaven head and offered sympathy.

'Give it a couple of days and no one'll notice,' said Doss.

Spiff stroked his bristles and shrugged. 'I don't care.'

'It doesn't look too bad,' said Skelly. 'Any road, you don't need to bother combing it.'

'The thing is, not to let on you're bothered,' said Ray. He unscrewed his jar of Brylcreem. 'Have a bit of this if you want. Not too much. Just enough to cover your fingertips.' He stepped back to admire his quiff in the washroom mirror. 'After all,' he said, 'you've not got the sort of hair that wants much looking after.'

Sister Anna remained with us for only a month. We heard Sister Beryl reprimanding her for allowing us to listen to a variety programme on the radio and for failing to see that the bedroom lights were turned off by nine-thirty. She also complained that on the days Sister Anna took us to morning assembly we had been seen waving at the girls across the hall. 'They need to be watched,' she said fiercely. 'You don't know what those little monkeys will get up to next.'

One morning I was awakened by screams from the next bedroom and ran through to see Bobby Cairns crouched in a corner while Sister Beryl belaboured him with both hands. He had wet his bed and tried to conceal what he had done by pulling the blankets over the drenched sheet and mattress. Now the blankets were on the floor and the sheet was wedged between Bobby and the wall.

Sister Beryl grabbed the front of his night-shirt with one hand and hit him repeatedly with the other. I saw her gold ring falling like a flail and blood on Bobby's face. Curds of spittle flew from her mouth and her spectacles dangled from one ear. She was panting as if she was nearing exhaustion, but the blows continued to rain down. Each one was accompanied by an exclamation which gave it extra impetus. *'Dirty! Filthy! Deceitful* boy!' Bobby tried to curl into a ball, but he was dragged to his feet and held at arm's length. There was a patch of urine on his night-shirt like a huge grease stain.

Tears and snot streaked his face and his nose was bleeding.

'Pick up your sheet,' ordered Sister Beryl. 'Take it with you so they can all see what a disgusting little beast you are.' She spun him round and pushed him on to the landing. 'Go on,' she said, 'get moving.' He bolted downstairs, his bare feet leaving damp prints on the uncarpeted boards, and she followed him, boxing his ears and jabbing him in the small of the back. She pursued him to the kitchen where she draped the wet sheet over his head. 'You can stand there while everyone else has their breakfast,' she said. 'Then you can do your own laundry. Nobody else wants to handle your filth.' She stood watching him, her chest heaving, her hair in wisps over her forehead. 'Go on the rest of you,' she said. 'Attend to your own business. Leave this little monkey where he is.'

Half an hour later when we took our places at table we realised that Bobby was no longer at his post. I looked in the washroom and found him bathing his nose while Sister Anna pummelled his sheet in a bath of hot water. There was a step behind me and I turned to see Sister Beryl.

'What's going on here?' she demanded.

Sister Anna wrung the sheet into a long corkscrew. 'You

can see what's going on.'

'I told him he had to wash that sheet himself.'

'And I told him that I'd do it,' said Sister Anna. 'He's in no fit state. He should be in the infirmary.'

'Should he indeed! And since when have you been a medical expert?'

'Long enough.' Sister Anna shook out the sheet and hung it over the side of the bath. 'I think his nose may be broken,' she said.

'Nonsense.'

'See for yourself. It's badly swollen. I think the nurse should have a look at it.'

Bobby Cairns remained where he was, his head bent over the washbasin. Ropes of bloody mucus hung from both nostrils. 'If he gave it a blow he'd look a lot better,' said Sister Beryl. Her words were as assertive as ever, but she sounded slightly querulous as though she blamed Bobby for the state he found himself in. Then she seemed to notice me for the first time. 'And what are you poking your nose in for? It's none of your business.'

'It's everyone's business,' said Sister Anna.

'I beg your pardon.' Sister Beryl's eyes opened wide in astonishment.

'It's certainly my business what happens to these children. I can't stand by and see a child bullied like this.'

'Not bullied. Reprimanded.' Sister Beryl changed colour as she spoke. Her colour ebbed away, leaving her bottom lip like a mauve blister tacked to the pale face. 'You want to be careful what you're saying,' she advised. 'There's such a thing as slander. I have witnesses.'

'Not me,' I said.

'Oh no, not you! We know about you. Expelled from one school and likely to be expelled from another.'

'I can't wait,' I said.

Sister Beryl slapped my face. 'Cheeky monkey!' She wheeled round on Sister Anna. 'Don't think I don't know what's going on here. I'm not blind. All those romps in the bedrooms. You must think I'm stupid.'

'I've no idea what you mean.' Sister Anna dried her hands on her apron. 'I think we should discuss this with Mr Buller.'

'And so do I . Right after assembly. I'll telephone him now.'

The open hostilities ended there. Sister Beryl and Sister Anna spent a full hour in Mr Buller's office and two days later Sister Anna left to become senior Sister in a house at the far end of the branch. 'I asked to go,' she told me weeks later when I was sweeping the road outside her front gate. 'There was no point in staying on and squabbling. That would have been no help to anyone.'

'What did Mr Buller say?' I asked.

'Nothing really. He said he wouldn't listen to any accusations, they just created bad feeling. When I tried to tell him what had happened he did this.' Sister Anna clapped her hands over her ears and laughed. 'Hear no evil.'

'That's not fair.' I felt cheated, as though Mr Buller had done me out of my emotional dues. I wanted to see Sister Beryl punished and Sister Anna exonerated, but I was beginning to realise that institutions did not work in such a straightforward way. Appearances had to be maintained. By moving Sister Anna on to where she was happy Mr Buller had lessened the likelihood of her making a formal complaint. Sister Beryl remained in charge at Mosscrop and although her temper was still peevish there had been no further violence; no more boys had been beaten.

'I know it's not fair,' said Sister Anna. 'But things are better, aren't they!'

I scratched some mud off my boots with the broom. 'I suppose so.'

'How are you getting on with Sister Joyce?'

'All right, I suppose.'

Sister Joyce was Sister Anna's replacement. She was new to the branch and with no advance reputation to guide us we were still making up our minds about her. It was not easy. She was demonstrably loyal to Sister Beryl, but she did not join in her bursts of shrill abuse. She enforced the rules, but invented none of her own. She did not insist on silence in the bedrooms, even after lights out. She did not loom behind us when we were washing. She kept her distance while we weighed each other up.

She was unlike any woman I had previously known. Before joining the Homes she had taught Physical Education at a girl's school and she moved like an athlete, treading springily and jerking open doors as if impatient to be off and running. She had short, flaxen hair, as bright as cellophane. Her calf muscles bulged beneath her stockings like tennis balls. She gave an impression of speed and compactness and taking no nonsense from anyone. One day she saw me in the yard showing Doss how to box. My knowledge was rudimentary, but at the Bluecoat school I had been a member of my house team and I at least knew the basic rules – how to lead with my left, how to counter-punch, how to feint and how to guard my face and body.

'Don't cross your legs when you move back,' I told him. 'Otherwise they can just push you over. And keep moving. If you stand still you're a target.'

We shuffled around the asphalt, squinting over our gloves. Doss aimed a wild swing at me and I dodged out of the way. 'You telegraphed your punch,' I said. 'Don't look at your glove when you're going to use it. Do it like this.'

I feinted at his jaw with my left and when he covered up I hit him in the stomach. His breath came out in a rush and he fell back against the wall. 'I'm out of puff,' he said. 'Let's have a rest.'

'I'll take over,' said Sister Joyce.

I grinned at her uncertainly. 'You're going to fight me?'

'Not fight,' she said. 'Box.'

'Do you know how?'

She pulled on the gloves that Doss had been wearing and held them out to Skelly to knot the laces around her wrists. 'Don't worry about me,' she said. 'Just carry on with the lesson.'

'You're sure?'

'Quite sure.' She adopted a fighter's crouch and before I could move she tapped me on the forehead, on the nose and on the chin as briskly as if she was knocking on a door. When I went after her she did it again. 'Am I crossing my legs?' she enquired. 'It used to be a bad habit of mine. I was always being ticked off for it.'

'Where was that?'

'At college.' She jabbed at my face and when I covered it with my gloves, punched me in the solar plexus. I heard someone laugh and tried to ignore it. 'We tried to form a women's boxing squad,' said Sister Joyce. 'The trouble was, there weren't any other women to fight and no men would take us on. They said it wasn't done.' She broke through my guard with a straight left and followed it with a right cross.

I picked myself up and slowly dusted my gloves. I had not landed one punch and the prospect of doing so seemed remote. 'You should be giving the lesson,' I said. 'Somebody else can have my turn.'

Boxing was not the only subject in which Sister Joyce excelled. The following Wednesday morning she watched us polishing our strips of floor and as I was about to lift the chairs down from the table she took one from my hands and holding it as she would a dancing partner, she waltzed the length of the room. At the far wall she spun round and waltzed back. 'I didn't mark the floor. I'm wearing slippers,' she said. 'It's lovely for dancing.'

'Fat chance of that,' I said.

'Are you interested?'

'I've never been taught.'

'Would you like to learn? Would any of the others?'

'I don't know.' I was not sure what I was getting myself into and I was reluctant to speak on anyone else's behalf. 'They might think it was a bit soft.'

'Is that what I am? Soft?'

'Not a bit,' I said truthfully. It was the last word I would ever apply to Sister Joyce.

'In the first place,' she went on, ticking off her fingers, 'dancing is good exercise. It also improves your manners and it teaches you how to get on with other people.' She drummed her fingers on the top of the lockers. 'It's Dancing Club tonight. Victor Sylvester on the wireless. Why don't we have a class here.'

'How about Sister Beryl?'

'She can join in.'

'I'll see what the lads think,' I said.

They were all in favour, except Spiff – who although indifferent to the merits of exercise and etiquette and sociability – acknowledged that dancing did at least give us direct access to girls. It was an argument we found irresistible.

'Just think of it,' said Ray, closing his eyes and clasping an imaginary partner.

'Get in there!' said Skelly.

Ray grabbed the lapels of his jacket and showed him his fist. 'Less of that. It's my lass you're talking about.'

'All right, all right. I didn't say anything about her.'

'Mind you don't.'

There was a convention we all observed that however itchy and lustful we felt towards girls in general, our official crushes – Gladys in Ray's case, Sadie in mine – were beyond vulgar gossip. They represented true love. We were allowed to boast about how far they let us go, to point to our swollen lips and the love bites on our necks. But it was all in the name of romance. Envy and speculation were permitted, indeed they were encouraged. But ribaldry was out; there was nothing funny about being stuck on someone. Ray kept a handkerchief belonging to Gladys in his breast pocket. It still smelled faintly of Soir de Paris. I had a garter which had kept up one of Sadie's stockings. We wore them like favours and slept with them under our pillows.

Our only partner at our first dancing class, however, was Sister Joyce. We had to learn the steps before we could inflict ourselves on strangers, she said. And Sister Beryl had a headache. 'What I want you to do,' Sister Joyce told me, 'is write down the instructions when they read them out on the wireless. Then we'll have them, chapter and verse, for practice later on.'

I did as I was asked but I could see no connection between the broadcast description of a quickstep and the dance itself which Sister Joyce demonstrated, spinning briskly between the tables humming to herself. 'It's a nice tune,' she said. '"Dancing on my Heart."' She stretched out her arms. 'Try it with me.'

I stumbled after her, trying to match the tempo but hobbled by embarrassment. 'We have to dance as one,' she said. 'Hold me closely.'

It was not like holding a girl. She had a hard, flat chest and her footwork, although it followed the Sylvester code, did not belong in a ballroom. She could have been playing tennis or doing physical jerks. I was aware of each of her muscles, perfectly tuned and buzzing with fitness. What I missed was the intimacy and yearning that the music implied.

'Next one,' she called and tugged Skelly on to the floor.

They were still dancing when Mr Buller arrived. He beckoned me into the sitting room where he sank into an armchair and drew a cigarette from his silver case. He tapped the end of it on his thumbnail and lit it carefully. 'How are you getting on?' he asked.

I darted a glance at Sister Beryl. 'Very well, thank you sir.'

'Is that right, Sister?'

'Well enough. He's been better behaved lately.'

Mr Buller bowed his head in approval and, as always, my eye was caught by his parting which ran like a pink seam through his yellow hair. I tried to concentrate on the smoke spinning from the tip of the cigarette and on the bare backs of the chairs, no longer concealed by Mrs King's embroidery. I heard the music next door change to a tango.

'Do you like dancing?' asked Mr Buller.

'I don't know how to do it yet.'

He waved his hand and the column of smoke collapsed like a falling chimney. 'It will come,' he said. 'All the social graces. But what about the rest of your life? What do you intend to do with it?'

'I don't know, sir.'

'No idea at all?'

'Not really, sir.'

'Strange. A boy like you.' Mr Buller leaned back and crossed his legs. The firelight twinkled on his brogues and he blew a smoke ring at the ceiling. 'Are you sorry you left your last school?'

'I didn't have much to do with it, sir.'

Mr Buller cleared his throat. 'We won't go into that. But do you miss the lessons, the subjects you don't get now?'

'I miss the languages,' I said. 'French and German.'

Mr Buller flipped his cigarette into the fire. 'What if you had the chance to take them up again? How would you feel about that?'

My heart stopped, then started again as if something had momentarily clogged a vein. I remembered what Ray had told me about Mr Buller liking to show off his bright lads. 'I'd like it very much, sir,' I said.

Mr Buller made a steeple of his fingers and lined me up in his sights. 'You're sure about that?'

'Positive, sir.'

'You won't let me down?'

'No sir.'

'Very well.' Mr Buller put out his hand and allowed me to shake it. 'You're going to Darwen Grammar School, starting next term.'

I felt a smile creep over my face, tilting the corners of my mouth and flooding my eyes. I was absurdly happy. I had been reprieved.

Sister Beryl jogged my elbow. 'Haven't you forgotten something?'

'What?' I could barely focus on her I was so excited.

'Say thank you to Mr Buller.'

'Thank you sir,' I said.

'Courtesy costs nothing,' said Sister Beryl. 'Let's hope they teach you that where you're going.'

Five

WE TRAVELLED to Darwen by train. It was a small mill town, not far from Blackburn, with a market, two cinemas and a paint factory. The moors swooped down on either side and tram lines scored the main road, impaling cobbles, shops and offices on rods of bright steel. To the west the town was overlooked by the Victoria Tower, built on the occasion of Queen Victoria's Jubilee, and on the opposite promontory stood Darwen Library which sparkled like frost when the sun glanced off its granite walls.

To catch the train we could either take the bus to Turton station or walk to Entwhistle, further up the line. Entwhistle was close to the viaduct over which the Northern Flier bustled towards bigger towns and urgent business. Our own travel was more restricted. But to walk through the station gate and board the train to school was like being granted a ticket of leave. The carriages were grimy and so cramped that our knees touched when we sat opposite each other. Sepia views of Blackpool and Morecambe lined the walls. Bouncing or even sitting heavily on the seat released clouds of dust. The heating was usually turned on, producing a smell of toasted wool with an underlying fragrance of oil. They were smells which reminded me both of home and of journeys to another school. But this time was different. I sensed prison doors bursting open. They did not vanish, but I was now able to pass through them. I was no longer confined.

In the mornings the train was full of men and women going to work. Each carriage was packed with mill hands and shift workers from factories where they made munitions. Thermos flasks jutted from their shoulder bags and hand-rolled cigarettes sagged from their lips. It was difficult to see across the compartment for smoke. They talked about football and pigeons and scant rations and how their sons and nephews were getting on in the forces.

'You'll not have long to go,' said one of the men, looking me up and down.

'If they'll have me,' I said. 'I strained my heart playing football.' I made up the lie on the spur of the moment, not because I wished to attract sympathy, but I looked years older than my age and I imagined that people might think I was dodging my call-up.

The morning and afternoon journeys were entirely different. The morning train was crowded and in the presence of adults we were subdued. We were too easily identified as children from the Homes to escape notice and any conduct which could be construed as unruly always found its way back at third or fourth hand, usually with embellishments which worsened in the telling.

In the afternoons, though, we had the train to ourselves. Cantering up the stone-flagged tunnel which led to the platform at Darwen station we would stop suddenly to hear the echo of our footsteps following us a fraction of a second behind. We were often late – delayed by a slow tram or loitering over the fiction shelves in the Library – and the train would be already waiting, steam seething up from the boiler, a porter glancing at his watch and urging us on as if there was a race to be won.

Whoever was first in the carriage was entitled to bag his place in the luggage rack. We considered it boring to make use of the seats and as soon as we had passed the signal box we hoisted ourselves up level with the communication cord, taking our ease in an unofficial hammock. It was not comfortable. Now and then our feet went through the netting. Once the entire rack collapsed and I fell on to the heads of the boys sitting beneath me. I never learned how the custom began or who started it. But there was prestige in travelling horizontally like a parcel. It was unorthodox, it was exciting and it was unobserved.

We set great stock on our privacy. Going to school for five

days of the week did not divorce us from the branch. On Saturdays we still had to report for duty at the Shop and although we were granted special dispensations for homework or school games after hours we still had to conform to the timetable of the house. We were constantly reminded that we were unusually privileged and that with privilege came reponsibility.

Sister Beryl, in particular, underlined the point again and again. She made a practice of sniffing my blazer as soon as I returned home to see if it smelled of tobacco smoke. 'Just let me catch you with cigarettes,' she threatened. 'You'll be straight over the road to see Mr Buller.'

She also went through my pockets when my jacket was hanging in the cloakroom, but I made certain there was nothing for her to find. Ray had already warned me what to expect. 'If you've got stuff you don't want her to see, take care you don't bring it in the house.' I took heed of the warning and made a hiding place in an old privy in the yard. The privies were no longer in use since inside lavatories had been installed. They were cold and stinking cells, visited only during games of King of the Castle. The bricks were loose and by prying one free I made myself a small safe deposit in which I stowed sweets, cigarettes and money, most of which I accumulated by selling my dinner tickets at cut price to my class mates at Darwen and filling up on chips and balm cakes which we bought in shops near the school.

I still travelled with Ray on the bus to the station, but I now had a new set of friends. There was Ernie Marsden, slow, mild and moon-faced, who was methodically reading his way through the novels of Thomas Hardy; a crop-headed boy named Dando who had a reputation as a swot; and Harry Barnes, a year older than me, whose skill as a shop-lifter established him in all our eyes as a super-criminal, as dashing as Raffles, as gallant as Robin Hood. Usually he worked alone, but if the enterprise called for two he would sometimes invite me to be his accomplice.

He had a favourite shop, a confectioners and

tobacconists, which was attended by one old lady. She spent most of the day in the back parlour and took her time in answering the shop bell. There was a high counter painted green and when we entered the shop, while I waited cash in hand to buy a packet of biscuits or a sherbet sucker, Harry would crouch at my feet, hidden from view, until the purchase had been made and I was safely outside. He would wait until the parlour door closed and then crawl behind the counter to loot the shelves. An average haul would include a full carton of cigarettes, chocolate and sweets which he would stow into his satchel and then creep back to the the other side of the counter. All he then had to do was open the street door so the bell rang and be ready and waiting to greet the old lady when she came out to serve him.

We were not troubled by conscience. It was no concern of ours that the shop-keeper could not afford to lose stock. 'She'll be covered by insurance,' said Harry as he gnawed a Milky Way in the train going home. 'You've got to understand. Businesses protect themselves.'

I was not altogether convinced, but it was a convenient argument to adopt and Harry delivered it with absolute authority. It was his way. He had studied confidence as other people studied mathematics and he was already a graduate. His composure was enviable. He looked like a Red Indian, with thick, coppery skin, high cheekbones and hair, waxy with brilliantine, which he combed into a peak adding at least two inches to his height. All his gestures were studied. When he smoked he held his cigarette away from him between thumb and forefinger and even on days of bright sunshine he wore the collar of his raincoat turned up so that it framed his face and concealed the darns on his shirt.

He viewed the world with what I first took to be disdain, but what was actually a deep-seated apprehension. He was careful not to show his feelings. His expression rarely changed; he was neither enthusiastic nor downcast. His judgements were not only ruthless, but delivered with an indifference to the effect they might have which I found shocking. One of the girls who travelled with us to Darwen was named Beatrice Wilkinson. She had red hair and was slightly bandy. Harry affected to despise her, but she ignored his deprecating asides until one day as she was walking ahead of us along the road to the station he tugged my sleeve and pointed to her bowed legs. 'She walks like she's got a worm up her cunt,' he said loudly.

Beatrice Wilkinson spun round, her face crimson. But Harry went on walking. It was as if the words had never been uttered and the insult was something we had all imagined.

'You shouldn't say that,' I told him.

Harry marched straight ahead. 'Why not? It's true.'

'That's not the point.'

'You've said the same thing.'

'Not so she could hear.'

'You still think it.'

There was a difference, I insisted. There was a gulf between what one thought and what one said. Beatrice's feelings had been needlessly hurt and no one had gained an advantage. 'What if she poked fun at your spots,' I said.

Harry looked at me pityingly. 'I won't always have spots. She'll always be bandy.' It was all the justification he needed.

The headmaster of the grammar school was named Hector ffoulkes Gaskell. He was dark and parched, with a purple jawline and a dusting of scurf on his shoulders. He wore a gown which was torn in several places as if it had been clawed by a giant cat and the first time we met I noticed that his shoes were encased in rubber galoshes. He saw me studying them and concernedly peeled them off. 'I always forget,' he explained. 'Not that it matters. Appearance is skin deep. What we have to build is character.'

I was placed in Form IVB, the same form I had been in at the Bluecoat school, but the syllabus was vastly different.

To my horror I discovered that I was expected to learn physics and that while French was taught, Latin was preferred to German.

'Spurs to achievement,' said Mr Gaskell. 'Obstacles are there to be overcome.'

I did not find it as easy as he assumed. Mathematics and algebra continued to baffle me and physics, I discovered, combined the worst elements of both. I was expected to study Latin in my free time in an attempt to catch up with the rest of the class, but after several weeks I decided that the battle was already lost. Instead, I chose to concentrate on the subjects in which I knew I could dazzle. In the half-term examinations I came top in History, Art and English Language and Literature. My written French was poor but in the oral test I received Mr Gaskell's special commendation, not for my accuracy in translation but for my confidence in reading without a pause a complete page of the New Testament in French.

It was Mr Gaskell's own method of doubling up on tuition. He never went so far as to say that he thought religious instruction a waste of time, but he was less concerned with the happenings in distant Galilee than in our ability to understand them in another language. The New Testament in French met all his requirements and the last phase of my spiritual education became a brisk trot through the gospels, an exercise for which I was uniquely well prepared, thanks to the Bible stories with which I had been regaled by my father – a lay preacher and student of Holy Writ.

Mr Gaskell also used the RI periods – two hours on Friday afternoons – to expand our knowledge of English poetry. He had a habit of pouncing on some unsuspecting youth, already planning how he would spend the weekend, and designating him as next week's lecturer. 'Your subject,' Mr Gaskell might tell him, 'is "The Rime of the Ancient Mariner". Read it, understand it and prepare a summary including a life of the poet with appropriate quotations.'

It was a task which few measured up to. Poetry was not the natural fare of Form IVB and however Mr Gaskell tried to impress on us the vitality and range of English verse, the response was disappointing. 'Does any one of you actually *enjoy* poetry?' he pleaded one afternoon. 'Any poem? Even a limerick.'

Without thinking, I put up my hand – the only one rash or vain enough to do so – and Mr Gaskell beamed his approval. 'Excellent,' he said. 'Now choose a poem which you think the rest of the class will enjoy. Try and convince them that poetry can be as exciting as your favourite comic, whatever that might be. Persuade them it's nothing to be afraid of.'

Looking around me I realised it was easier said than done. Form IVB had already vetoed Wordsworth and all that Keats's 'Ode to a Nightingale' had yielded was one line – 'My heart aches and a drowsy numbness pains my sense' – which was quoted whenever an unpopular lesson drew near. After much agonising I decided to give a dramatic presentation of one of my favourite poems, *Reynard the Fox*. The narrative was thrilling and easy to follow, there was a happy ending when the fox escaped the hounds, and the poet himself was still alive, not mouldering respectably in Westminster Abbey. Even the poet's name, John Masefield, sounded ordinary. You could imagine it on a shop front or on the side of a van.

I chose what parts of the poem I would recite and which parts I would condense into passages of linking prose. I wrote a brief account of Masefield's life, emphasising his hard times and his spell on a wind-jammer that had rounded Cape Horn. I carefully included the fact that he had dared to use swear words in his poems – words which in any other context were still taboo. And after five minutes of ritualistic shuffling, desk lids being banged and throats being cleared, a rare and beautiful silence fell. I looked up from my book and saw twenty-four pairs of eyes fixed on me. It was my first captive audience. I could make them gasp and I could make them cry. They did not want the poem to end. I drew a deep breath and savoured the moment. The sense of power was intoxicating.

When it was over I received Mr Gaskell's congratulations with what I hoped was fitting modesty. The triumph, I wanted to imply, was Masefield's. But I had no intention of refusing a decent measure of credit. It was not everyone who could make poetry popular. I was not sure how I could make use of the reputation but as I had already learned, credit rarely came amiss.

A tall, bony boy wearing horn-rimmed spectacles and with a forehead so shiny that it seemed to have been polished with a silk duster asked if he could borrow my copy of Masefield. 'I'm none so keen on the poetry, but I like animals,' he explained.

His name was Philip Watson and he planned to become a vet. His father was a mill foreman and his mother ran a small bakery in the town. She had two ovens at the back of the house and there was a shop at the front in which she sold bread and fancy cakes. The Watsons lived over the shop.

'You can come for tea if you like,' said Phil. 'Cheer me up while I do my piano practice.'

Learning to play the piano was his mother's idea. She was as neat as a bun with scrubbed and busy hands and a fixed idea that it was her duty to lovingly hound her family in the pursuit of excellence. Phil was the first person I had ever met who actually disliked music. He was not seduced by melody. He could not remember a tune and his playing was painfully stilted. He persisted in his efforts because his mother threatened to stop his pocket money if he gave up and also because he knew how dearly she longed for him to develop what she believed to be his natural gift. She was mistaken but would not be persuaded otherwise.

'It'll dawn on her one day,' said Phil as he perched himself glumly on the piano stool. 'But think of all the time I'll have wasted sitting here.'

To please me he played a song called 'Five O'Clock Whistle' which was currently popular and no part of his official repertoire. He gave me a hard look when I sung along. 'You know the words without reading the music,' he said accusingly.

I beat time on top of the piano. 'I've heard it on the wireless.'

'Better there than here,' said Phil, plodding on to the end of the piece.

Mrs Watson invited me to stay with them for the weekend. I asked Sister Beryl who referred me to Mr Buller, who – to the surprise of both of us – said yes. 'Just mind you behave yourself,' she said as I packed the clean shirt she gave me. 'And don't think you're something special just because you've got posh friends.'

'They're not posh,' I said. 'Nothing like.'

'Any friends outside would be posh for some of the boys here,' said Sister Beryl.

I knew what she meant but I did not reply. I was afraid that, even in the face of Mr Buller's blessing, she would find a reason for keeping me at Mosscrop.

'And I want you back here Sunday afternoon,' she said. 'In time for the evening service.'

I saw the bus make its turn, ready to take us to the station, and grabbing my satchel I ran to catch it. Sister Beryl watched me through the dining-room window and I could still sense her scrutiny as we drove away down the hill.

It was strange, being in an ordinary house again. There was scented soap and soft towels in the bathroom. There was a copy of the *Radio Times* beside the wireless. I was told to help myself to sugar from a bowl on the table instead of seeing it tipped into the pot before my cup was filled. I was served a boiled egg for my tea. 'I hope you like it runny,' said Mrs Watson. 'That's how we do them here.'

'Lovely,' I said.

'And leave room for some plum jam. I expect you can manage that.'

I ate in silence, savouring every morsel. Between

mouthfuls I kept my hands in my lap and was careful not to rest my feet on the rung of my chair. The shop bell pinged and Mrs Watson straightened her apron and went to see to the customer. 'You want to watch it,' said Phil. 'You'll be showing me up if you're not careful.'

'How do you mean?'

'Are you always as good as this?'

I choked on a crumb. 'As good as what?'

'Your halo's showing.' He clapped me on the back. 'Have a sup of tea,' he advised. 'You've gone all red.'

I shared Phil's bedroom in the attic. There were twin beds. The walls were plastered with photographs of film stars and footballers and leaning in one corner was an air-rifle. 'We can go shooting tomorrow if you like,' he said.

'What do you get?'

'Sparrows mostly. That's in the allotment. Or we could try the sewage works. There's thousands of starlings there.' He passed me the gun. 'Don't squeeze the trigger when it's not loaded. You'll spoil the spring.'

I poked the gun through the open skylight and aimed it at the Victoria Tower on the far side of the town. The Watsons' shop was in a street behind the station and between us and the memorial lay terraces of roof-tops, descending rows of chimneys and a gulf of air, as blue as tobacco smoke. 'Sometimes that tower looks so close you could reach out and touch it,' said Phil. 'It's where courting couples go. If you had field glasses you could see them from here.'

'Not to see them doing anything.'

'If the glasses were strong enough.'

'You'd need army glasses.'

'That's what I meant,' said Phil. 'The sort they have on manoeuvres.'

'What sort of manoeuvres?'

'Any sort,' said Phil. 'Use your imagination.'

We remained looking out of the skylight until it was dark. The sun crept behind a mill chimney and slid down the other side. The blue of the air deepened like a flannel soaking up water and from far across the moors we heard curlews calling.

'There's good nesting there,' said Phil. 'I've stopped taking eggs though. It doesn't seem right.'

'Why not?'

'I don't know. They go to so much bother, it's not fair.'

I watched the stars through the skylight until I fell asleep and I was awakened in the morning by the smell of fresh bread and the sound of sharp, peremptory tapping in the street below. It went on for several minutes and Phil opened his eyes. 'It's not for us,' he said. 'Go back to sleep.'

'What is it?'

'Just the knocker-up. He's waking folks on early shift.'

I peered out of the skylight and between the gables caught sight of a man carrying a long pole. As I watched he hoisted it to his shoulder and rapped on the bedroom window of the house opposite. The curtains twitched and he moved on to the house next door. I climbed back into bed and dozed until I heard a curious clattering in the street as if a carpet of steel rings was being dragged along the pavement.

Phil opened one eye. 'Clogs,' he said succinctly. 'Folks going to work.'

I watched them pass below, saluting each other on the corner, cap brims tugged down, their shoulders hunched against the early chill. The town was a well of mist, but sunlight gilded the Victoria Tower so that it shone like a pillar of fire. There was a high wind which shredded the cloud into strips of cirrus, but between it the sky was a bright enamelled blue.

'Is it time to get up?' I asked.

Phil held his watch at arm's length. 'It's not seven yet.'

'Is it too early then? There's someone in the bakehouse.'

'It's our lasses. They have to be there.' His voice was faint and he lay perfectly still as if convalescing from sleep.

'What lasses?'

'*Our* lasses. Mary and Jean. They work in the shop.'

'Lets go and see them.' I wanted the day to begin. Every second I spent in bed meant that time was going to waste.

Phil yawned and slowly converted the yawn into a sigh. 'Saturday morning and you want to be up already.' He rolled back his sheets an inch at a time as if reluctant to yield to the day.

'All right then.' He planted his bony feet on the floor and wiggled his toes. 'You can have the bathroom first. Your towel's the one with a pink edge.'

'You're not going back to bed?'

Phil pointed to his feet. 'Once they're out, I'm up. Go on, make haste.'

We washed and dressed and went downstairs. With each step the smell of baking bread grew stronger and when Phil opened the door of the bakehouse I was enveloped in a gust of hot yeasty air which crisped my skin and made my mouth water. Two girls wearing loose white overalls were stacking loaves in wooden trays. They both looked about twenty. Mary was fair and Jean was dark, but their hair was tucked under elasticated caps and only stray wisps escaped to frame their flushed faces.

'Look what the cat's dragged in,' said Mary. 'What's up then? Couldn't you sleep?'

Phil jerked his thumb at me. 'It's his fault. He wanted to say hello.'

'Is that right?' said Jean.

I nodded, quite unable to speak. Beneath their overalls they appeared to be wearing very little. I saw the edge of a slip, a shoulder indented by a satin strap, the soft notch of a pair of breasts, and I was struck dumb. Their bare arms were dusted with flour and when Jean straightened her cap her hand left a white smudge on her forehead. 'Say hello if you're going to,' she said.

I smiled foolishly. 'Hello.'

'He can talk then,' said Mary.

'When he likes,' said Phil.

Mary put her arm around Jean's waist and together they closed in on me. I did not know where to look and stared desperately at the floor. 'Is he shy?' asked Jean.

Mary put her hand under my chin and tilted my face

upwards. 'Are you,' she said. 'Is that what's wrong?'

I shook my head. 'Not really.'

'It's us then,' she said. 'He's overcome by our beauty.'

They threw back their heads and laughed. I could see their bodies shaking beneath their overalls and suddenly I smelled sweat, not pungent but tangy and fresh like a scent which hard work had unstoppered. I saw it beading their upper lips and imagined it clinging like dew to the fleece beneath their arms. Their throats pulsed like birds singing. A dark curl, coiled like a watch spring, escaped from beneath Jean's cap. They stood on either side of me and linked their free hands, caging me between them.

'Daft lasses,' said Phil. 'Leave him be. We're going to have our breakfast.'

They released me, still laughing, and waved us through the door. 'Are they always like that?' I asked.

'Daft, you mean?'

'No. Do they always dress like that?'

'They always wear overalls and caps. My mother says they have to.'

'But underneath . . .'

Phil looked at me blankly. 'Underneath what?'

'Underneath the overalls. They had almost nothing on.'

'Oh, that.' He led me into the dining room. 'It's hot in there. They'd melt if they had their frocks on.' We sat at the table and he passed me the cornflakes.

'They're pretty,' I said.

'Pretty daft you mean.'

'No,' I said. 'Really pretty. Nice faces and that.' I realised I could not be more explicit. Phil had no idea what I was talking about. He had grown up with girls in the bake house. They were familiar objects; daft lasses. I could not begin to describe to him how exciting I found them, how the thought of touching them made me tremble.

'They're all right,' he conceded. 'For lasses, I mean.'

After breakfast we went to the sewage works and shot starlings as they rode on the sprinklers slowly rotating over the filter beds. Each sprinkler had room for about fifteen birds sitting wing to wing, fluting and gargling until a slug from the air-rifle knocked them from their perch in a puff of feathers. When one bird fell another instantly took its place. It was like potting targets pegged to a roundabout. When we had shot six Phil called a halt. 'I'd better pick them off the filters,' he said. 'The gaffer gets narky if they're left there. He says they pollute the water, or something.'

'He's not to know we shot them,' I said.

'He'll know.'

'How's that' I asked.

'I never wing them,' said Phil. 'I kill them stone dead. I don't like causing them pain. And then there's the tally.'

'What's that?'

'I collect their legs to show how many I've killed. One leg from each bird.' He took a clasp knife from his pocket and tested the blade with his thumb. 'It's all right,' he said. 'They can't feel anything now.'

That evening we went to the wrestling at Blackburn Baths. We caught the tram outside Woolworths and collared a front seat upstairs. The top deck was the place to ride. A smell of ozone blew through the window as sparks showered from the arm that clasped the wires and when we turned corners the entire tram heeled over like a galleon cuffed by a gale.

'I reckon this one's top-heavy,' said Phil as we tilted more drastically than usual towards the pavement.

'D'you think we might crash?'

'Happen,' he said. 'It's been known.'

Scaring ourselves with possible disasters added to the pleasure of the outing. It was even better after dusk when we swooped through dimmed rows of street lights, like a night fighter diving through streams of flak. The target lay straight ahead. Nothing could stop or divert us. To complete the mission was all that mattered. We wound down the windows and narrowed our eyes in the slip-stream.

'You'll freeze folk to death,' said the conductor, winding them up again. 'What are you? Grammar-school lads? You should know better.'

At the Baths we joined the queue at the box office. Phil tugged my sleeve and indicated a figure standing at a pie stall on the opposite corner. 'It's him,' he said. 'It's Ernie Baldwin.'

'It's not.'

'It is,' he said. 'Look at the size of him.'

Ernie Baldwin was a heavyweight wrestler whose battles with The Farmer's Boy and Dirty Jack Pye were epics which thrilled us week after week although, as Phil's father had pointed out, it seemed curious how each contestant seemed to win in turn, thus keeping honours even. They also alternated their roles, sometimes playing tragic hero, sometimes blackest villain, as though their temperament and technique also changed by rote. Jack Pye, though, was unremittingly evil. No one employed such foul tactics. No one bit, or gouged, or pulled hair with such evident relish. Ernie Baldwin was fighting him this evening and I worried for his safety.

We watched respectfully while he bought three large meat and potato pies and lined them up on the counter of the stall. He picked up one pie between finger and thumb, lodged it neatly in his mouth, chewed for a count of ten and swallowed once. The second and third pie were dealt with in the same way. Ernie Baldwin's expression did not change. He looked like a man contemplating infinity.

'He's keeping up his strength,' said Phil.

'He'll bloody need it,' said the man in front of us. 'Pye's going to tear his bloody head off.'

We sat in the gallery, almost directly above the ring. The main body of the hall was in darkness and arc lamps blazing down on to the canvas drilled holes through the haze of tobacco smoke. I had never been to a wrestling match before. At school it was more popular than boxing because the PT master, brought out of retirement by the war, was a venerable athlete named Stiffy Stevenson who had once wrestled for Britain in the Olympics. 'I was called Tiger in those days,' he told us. He despised most of the new men in British wrestling, with the exception of the heavyweight champion, Bert Assirati. 'See him if you get the chance,' he advised. 'There's not many can touch him.'

My interest in the sport was also fired by the conversation of my friends. Every Monday morning there was a passionate inquest on the weekend's bouts. Holds were demonstrated, falls denounced. The most admired throw was the Irish whip, performed to perfection by the form hero, a clean-cut middle-weight, implausibly billed as Carlton Smith. His triumphs were ours. He was proof against whatever villainy his opponent could muster. When, after the two preliminary bouts, he strode up the aisle and vaulted into the ring my excitement was intense.

I leaned over the brass balustrade and admired the way his muscles rippled beneath his skin, like water flowing under a slick of oil. He had fair hair, cut short, and his trunks and his wrestling boots were royal blue. His opponent was named Charlie Foy, a stocky Irishman who removed his green robe with a flourish to reveal a harp-emblazoned leotard, stuffed with an abundance of wiry black hair. It was all his own, I realised, growing like brambles on his chest, his shoulders, his arms and his legs, so densely that no clear patch of skin remained visible.

When he was called to the centre of the ring he refused to shake hands and before the bell sounded, while Carlton Smith was still in his corner with his back turned, he had bounded across the intervening space to deliver a forearm smash to the nape of our hero's neck. Carlton Smith sagged to his knees. The timekeeper rang the bell and Charlie Foy continued his attack. He was hauled off by the referee, but to no avail; Smith was still down. Charlie Foy clamped both hands on either side of his neck and squeezed. His thumbs dug pits into the glowing flesh and I winced in sympathy. The grip was paralysing. No one could excape. And then the impossible happened. Slowly, valiantly Carlton Smith rose to his full height. He spread his arms, the tendons fluttering in his chest, and wielding his rigid hands like axe blades he chopped at Foy's hairy ribs.

The effect was dramatic. Foy reeled back towards his corner, gasping for breath. His mouth gaped open, his eyes bulged. Carlton Smith seized his right arm and yanked him to the centre of the ring. He swung the arm as if he was starting a tractor and Foy turned a complete somersault, landing flat on his back. The manoeuvre was repeated several times. The arms of the wrestlers seemed to be welded together, but then Carlton Smith released his hold. He stepped back, measured his distance and launched himself into the air, feet first. His royal blue boots connected with the point of Foy's jaw. Foy hit the canvas, his arms and legs spread-eagled, and lay there twitching while the referee counted him out.

'Easy,' said Phil.

'Too bloody easy,' said the man we had met in the queue. 'All over in one? That Carlton Smith must have a train to catch.'

The rest of the bouts followed much the same pattern and the verdict was usually predictable. Whoever initiated the dirty moves was punished in kind and then either pinned or forced to submit while the crowd roared its approval. There was a smell in the air not so much of blood, but retribution. Justice was being done on our behalf. When Jack Pye and Ernie Baldwin climbed through the ropes the fervour was almost evangelical. More than our sympathies were being enlisted. We were partaking of a ritual. Each of us had a part to play. We stamped our feet and drummed our fists on the sill of the balcony. We shredded our programmes and screwed the torn pages into balls which we hurled into the arena. As they entered the cone of light which seared the ring they seemed to burn like moths.

Jack Pye raked the paper pellets together and kicked them into the laps of the nearest spectators. He grinned into the darkness and clasped his hands over his head in a victory salute. 'There's your winner,' said the man from the queue.

'Never,' said Phil.

'Baldwin's not got a chance.'

'Of course he has,' I said.

The man from the queue rolled his eyes at the rafters. 'Experts!'

Pye had a dark, cropped head and shoulders which sloped down to his elbows. Baldwin was fair with a pink slightly puzzled face and a belly which divided into two distinct folds. I thought of the meat and potatoes digesting within its bulk and I was not comforted.

My fears were well founded. Pye dominated the fight from the start. He was cunning, wicked and inventive. His villainy was so blatant that it was funny; so audacious that I could hardly believe what I was seeing. It was like watching a film in which the master criminal announced his plans and then carried them out despite the pathetic attempts of the law to forestall him. While the referee was monitoring his application of a toe lock to Baldwin's left foot he was, at the same time, secretly crushing his windpipe with his knee. When Baldwin was jack-knifed with a punch to the stomach, Pye was protesting loudly that the blow had been delivered with the heel of his hand. He pulled hair, attacked while his opponent was outside the ring, advanced on him between rounds with a stool concealed behind his back, and finally spat water into his eyes, blinding him so that he failed to anticipate the forearm smash which felled him. It was another knockout.

I found myself hanging over the balcony, screaming at Baldwin to get up and fight. Phil grabbed my jacket and pulled me back into my seat. 'Steady on,' he said.

Sweat gummed my hair to my forehead. 'He needs telling.'

'You've told him already,' said Phil.

'I thought you wanted him to win.'

'Not that much. You'll get us chucked out.'

I subsided slowly. What I most wanted was to see the whole thing again or, failing that, a re-match in which the tables might conceivably be turned. I did not feel sorry for

Baldwin. He was too slow, too clumsy, too much of a victim. Pye was his executioner and he had carried out his commission. He was a rogue and a rule-bender, but he had kept faith by living up to his reputation. I felt my loyalties dissolve and re-form.

The man from the queue tapped me on the shoulder. 'I told you so.'

'Wait till next time.'

'Oh aye,' he said, stroking his chin. 'And pigs might fly.'

We rode back on the tram. The blackout was complete but the moon was up and the tram lines curved ahead of us, slicing through the cobbles like wire through cheese. 'Can you come again?' asked Phil.

'I'd like to,' I said. I had already decided that I would play down how much I had enjoyed my stay. It was unwise to show too much pleasure. Privileges granted could also be denied and I did not want my happiness used as a weapon against me.

Six

WE WERE NOT kept short of food at the Homes, but the diet was restricted because of wartime rationing and boring in a way peculiar to all institutions. During the winter we had porridge and stews; in the summer, a variety of salads which differed from each other only to the amount of grit which embossed the lettuce. A piece of cheese, a radish, a slice of fried bread were eagerly anticipated events. Our taste buds languished. We stared at our plates and craved excitement. One of the boys who worked on the farm brought home cow cake for us to eat and locusts which, at first, I imagined to be the insects described in the Bible but which turned out to be a kind of dried bean, surprisingly sweet and satisfying to palates starved of sugar.

We were willing to try anything. There was practically no fruit. Oranges, lemons and bananas had entirely vanished. The only apples which came to us from the stores were small and sour. Biting into one withered the mouth. Perversely, we ate sourdock for pleasure and young dandelion leaves, although Sister Beryl warned us they would make us wet our beds. We nibbled hawthorn buds and chervil from the ditches. One Saturday Mr King told us that our job for the morning was to cut kale for the farm cattle and, without warning, we discovered a new source of nourishment.

The kale plantation covered several acres behind Argyle House. It resembled a miniature jungle. The leaves were broad and dark green and usually pearled with rain-drops and the stalks – which the cows ate – were segmented like bamboo. It was a plant which looked too tropical to be growing on a hillside in Lancashire. We were issued with billhooks and slashers. A farm cart drew up on the verge of the meadow and we set to work. It was simple and repetitive. You gripped the stem, slashed at the base, hacked off the top and started a pile. At the end of the row you collected the pile and stacked it on the cart. After two minutes my jacket was drenched. On every side the kale bobbed and rippled like an inland sea. Heads dived down and reappeared. I saw Mr King leaning against the cart, the smoke from his freshly kindled pipe streaming away on the wind. The kale smelled like cabbage, but down among the stems there was a fresher, nuttier odour too. I inspected the segment I had just cut and raised it to my nose. It was firm and white inside and slick with juice. I dabbed it with my tongue and felt my mouth water. I peeled away the rind and took a bite. It was almost like eating coconut (something I had not tasted since Burslem Wakes before the war) and I filled my mouth. By the end of the morning I had devoured at least two stems and as we walked back to the Shop I heard my stomach rumbling.

'What are you eating?' asked Ray.

I showed him. 'Just some kale.'

'D'you think you're a cow or something? You need a special kind of digestion for that. They've got a double stomach, you know. We did it in biology.'

'He's right,' said Ernie Marsden. 'They sick it up and eat it twice.'

'I'm not bothered,' I said.

Ray tapped my belt buckle. 'You're making chamber music already. Wait till later.'

'Do you feel sick?' asked Ernie.

'Not a bit.'

'You will,' he said. 'Just mark my words.'

He was right, of course, although my nausea was induced more by what people said than what I had eaten. 'Next time you'll know better,' said Mr King. 'Kale is for cows. Happen you'll give us a couple of gallons later on.'

A great deal of our work on the Shop had to do with the production of food. When we grumbled, albeit quietly, we were told by Mr Buller that we formed part of the vast land army of Britain which was helping to fight the war. 'And win it,' he said fiercely. 'Think of this meadow, this valley as your front line. We all have to do our bit.' He made a speech of this sort at least once a week, drawing his inspiration from pamphlets issued by government departments. He took the war effort very seriously and saw himself as our commander in the field. It was not a performance which commanded much loyalty and we tended to waste food as a deliberate act of sabotage, aimed at undermining Mr Buller's campaign.

Our treason did not go unnoticed. 'Half Europe could live on what we throw away,' he thundered after poking through the swill buckets. 'I've a good mind to make you take all this back,' He impaled half a loaf on his walking stick and held it up for our inspection. 'You see this? Perfectly good bread. Thrown away here while people are starving.'

'It's mouldy, sir,' said Ray. 'It's all green on the back.'

Mr Buller took a closer look. 'Then it shouldn't be mouldy. That's wasteful too.' His pink face took on the fixed expression we had come to associate with the war and dedication and higher things. 'Think of food as ammunition,' he said. 'Don't put weapons into Hitler's hands.'

I reminded myself to look for that particular phrase in the month's pamphlets and tilted the bucket to catch the loaf as it fell from Mr Buller's stick. We were letting him down and he let us know it. Our response was inadequate. We were helping to lose the war. On bleak winter days we were dispatched to pick stones from moorland which had never been farmed before. Our haul ranged from small pebbles to glacial boulders which remained embedded in the peat, defying all our efforts to dislodge them. They too were Mr Buller's enemies. His daily round took on the aspect of a visit to the front line. Coat collar turned up, gum boots streaked with mud, he squelched through heather and cotton grass taking stock of the opposition.

'What about levering with a crowbar here, Mr King?'

'Wouldn't work, sir. Wrong angle.'

'Have we tried rocking it from side to side?'

'Sunk too deep, sir.'

'Dynamite?'

'None available, sir.'

The boulders leaned into the wind like Easter Island statues, remnants of older and darker times and Mr Buller, the new man, feared for his faith. It would not move mountains. It could not even shift a boulder weighing only a few tons. He despaired of us all.

He was happier training us in aircraft recognition at weekly parades of the Air Training Corps. All the older boys had volunteered to join because we were issued with uniforms and on Wednesday evenings we marched down to the village hall, our boots shining like black glass, our forage caps stuck at an impossible angle on the sides of our heads. Mr Buller also had a uniform made of fine barathea and from somewhere he had acquired a swagger stick with which he continuously slapped his thigh while the parade was shaping up.

He tried to recruit Mr King as a drill instructor but, surprisingly, his appeal was turned down. Officially it was because Mr King was needed at home to look after his wife. But the truth was that he had no time whatever for the ATC. We were Brylcreem boys in the making; Flash Harries whose glamour distracted the attention of folk who should know better. Wars were fought on the ground by soldiers and not in the air. They were also fought at sea, although there was something frivolous about men shooting at each other in boats. But the real battles, said Mr King, were land battles. 'Omdurman,' he said smugly. 'Wipers, Vimy Ridge.' The names meant little more to us than pictures in the bound editions of the *London Illustrated News* which Mr King kept in his sitting room below rows of paperback Western novels. I remembered drawings of troops scrambling from trenches, their bayonets fixed, led by a tin-hatted officer brandishing a revolver. I recalled photographs of dead men and mules and convoys of lorries stranded in fields of mud cratered by shell holes. On balance, I preferred my war to be glamorous. I did not want to die in dirt.

On our way back from ATC nights we marched smartly through the village and then broke ranks on the long road up to the Homes. If they could slip out unseen Sadie and Gladys waited for us in the spinney below Argyle House. They both admired our uniforms but Gladys complained that the material scratched her face when Ray clasped her to his chest. 'My skin's so delicate,' she said. 'It shows up every mark.'

'All over?' demanded Ray.

'Wouldn't you like to know.'

'Wouldn't you like to show me?'

She slapped his hand. 'Don't be in such a hurry.'

'They'll be looking for us,' said Sadie.

I turned her wrist to look at her watch. 'Not yet.'

'You don't know Sister Marion,' she said. 'She never lets us alone.'

'Quite right too,' said Ray. He pulled Gladys deeper into the spinney and we could hear them giggling behind the blackthorn.

'Will you miss me when I leave?' asked Sadie.

'It's not for a while is it?'

'Soon enough,' she said. Her voice took on the plaintive note I had learned to dread. It hinted at separation and the pain of parting. It was like the lyric of a song sung by Vera Lynn, but without the music it sounded faintly foolish.

I slid my fingers under the bottom of Sadie's jumper and felt her squirm away. 'Why not?' I asked.

'People might see.'

'What people?'

'People up at the house.' She jerked her head backwards and through the branches I saw heads protruding from the windows of Argyle House, all of them turned in our direction.

'What do they think they're doing?'

'Keeping watch,' said Sadie. 'They'll whistle if anyone comes.'

'They're too busy getting an eyeful.'

'If it worries you we'd better go.' She pulled down her jumper and smoothed her hair. 'I'm off, Gladys,' she called.

'Wait for me.' The bushes threshed and Gladys emerged, followed by Ray who was smiling broadly.

We kissed the girls, more passionately than usual in deference to the spectators above us, and waited until they had climbed the slope and turned into the yard. 'What's up?' said Ray. 'Is she giving you a bad time?'

'Not really.'

'You don't want to worry,' said Ray. 'She'll come round. They all do.'

He smiled reminiscently and I resolved not to ask him for details. He was already far too pleased with himself and I had no wish to bolster his complacency. Nor did I want to discuss what he assumed I was not getting. There were, in fact, girls in Darwen far more outgoing than Sadie, but I was not ready to describe my prospects to Ray. He made jokes which were not really jokes. He resented any hope or achievement which he could not better. He was jealous at even the hint of preferment. 'That Gladys,' he said, stroking his teeth. 'She really knows how to kiss.'

The Darwen girls fell into two main categories; those we met at school and the others who lay in wait for us in the town. Both groups regarded us as curiosities – princes or prisoners who could be courted or used without commitment. We did not belong to the same tribe and so we were not bound by the same rules. We did not live near by so we did not provoke neighbourhood gossip. We were valued for our rarity and our discretion. We were an indulgence anyone could afford.

There was a girl in my form named Doris Cooper who took to writing me passionate letters in green ink. Without preamble she told me that she loved me, that she lay awake at night thinking of me and that she had repeated my name four hundred times before falling asleep. I was rather startled. Not only were we not close to each other, but we had barely spoken. She was thin and excitable with a flushed face and straight brown hair. She was never alone, but formed part of a group which huddled in corners giggling loudly and trading secrets in shrill whispers. I felt them watching me as I entered a room but when I looked at them they turned their backs and the giggles intensified. If I remained where I was they would peep over their shoulders, their eyes bold and inviting, but if I made any move towards them they would scamper away, their laughter skirling behind them. Sometimes one would dart back and press yet another of Doris's letters in my hand and I would read it, aware that I was being watched and my reaction noted.

I always smiled because there was little else I could do. The notes were excessively fond, and deeply boring. They began with 'Darling' and ended in rows of kisses. They described feelings with a wealth of sentiment, but at the same time they were curiously unspecific. Apart from kissing, no physical activity was ever mentioned. The tone was fervent but chaste. They might have been written by an excited angel.

I knew that I was supposed to reply, but I did not know what to say. I studied the fat green characters which crammed the sheets of lined paper and wondered how to match the ardent, empty phrases. The language was as vacuous as the writing. Both had loops and curls which embellished instead of making plain. I asked the advice of Harry Barnes.

'Make it soppy,' he said.

'How?'

'Use the right words.' He listed them on the fingers of his left hand. 'Adore. Tender. Heart. Crush. Yearn. Don't try and make it fancy. Keep it simple. Doris Cooper reads the comics. It's what she's used to.'

'I can't write that stuff,' I protested.

'Anyone can.'

'I feel such a fool.'

'I'll help you,' said Harry. 'You never know your luck.'

'What do you mean?'

'Don't you know about Doris? Her dad's got a sweet shop. He keeps fags under the counter.'

'That's nothing to do with me,' I said.

Harry punched my shoulder in exasperation. 'It's to do with all of us. If you get the fags you can pass them round.'

'Fat chance,' I said.

'Don't you mess it up,' said Harry. 'Think of your pals.'

He was right as always. The following week I opened the lid of my desk and found a packet of Player's Bachelor hidden beneath my biology book. Two days later there was a packet of Sun Valley. I smiled my thanks across the classroom but Doris pretended not to see me.

'What's wrong with her?' I asked Harry.

'She doesn't want it to look like a bribe. Try and get her on her own. You can thank her then.'

'I can't get near her,' I said. 'She's always with her mates.'

'Write her a letter saying you have to see her. Make it really strong. Tell her you dream of kissing her soft lips.'

I shook my head in dismay. 'She'll never fall for that.'

'You're a twit,' said Harry. 'It's what she wants to hear.'

We wrote the letter during the morning break and I put it in Doris's satchel before the class reassembled. I saw her unfold the page and as she read it her face turned a vivid red as if dye had been pumped beneath her skin. She glanced across the classroom and nodded once.

I was elated but nervous too. Conversation with Doris Cooper presented problems I had never previously encountered. What she talked about with her girl friends was boys; how far they went, how far they should be permitted to go, what sort of husbands they would make and how much they looked like Robert Taylor or Tyrone Power. Sometimes they discussed parents, the iniquities of teachers and in which classes it was safe to wear makeup.

Boys were not required to hold opinions on such topics.

I looked covertly across the rows of desks to where Doris was writing on a small pad concealed within her exercise book, her tongue gripped between her teeth, her head cradled in the crook of her arm, and I realised with a sinking heart that she was composing yet another letter to me. It would be delivered before the lesson ended, travelling dangerously from hand to hand across the classroom, liable at any time to be intercepted and read aloud by the teacher in which case I thought, with almost a sense of relief, not only the coming rendezvous but possibly the whole affair would be aborted. But my hopes were dashed. The letter arrived declaring love undying, love unparalleled, love which Doris, the writer, found almost too much to bear. When I looked up our eyes met and she gave a brisk little nod of satisfaction as if the coal had been delivered or I had washed my hands as I'd been told to.

We had arranged to meet during the school dinner hour. Our meeting place was almost romantic: a lightning-riven oak beside a small pond which lay on neglected farm land opposite the school. A few cows stood behind hanks of barbed wire, their jaws rotating ceaselessly, and a pair of moorhens jerked in and out of the reeds fringing the pond. It was a day in late spring and buds were beginning to burst. The air smelled of sap and in spite of myself I felt a surge of excitment.

Doris stepped from behind a hawthorn. 'I've been waiting ages.'

'I'm sorry,' I said. 'I'm not late.'

'Did anyone see you?'

'Not that I know of. What does it matter anyhow?'

'I don't want folk talking.' She was wearing her blue school raincoat, buttoned all the way up to her neck and with the belt tightly cinched. She glanced nervously over her shoulder.

'They all knew we were meeting,' I said.

'You mean they're hidden somewhere watching us.'

'I didn't say that. I mean there's no point in pretending

we weren't going to see each other.'

'If me dad knew he'd kill me,' said Doris.

'What for? We're not doing anything.'

'We're not going to, neither,' she said sharply. 'It's just that people talk.'

I put my arm round her shoulder but she shied away. 'None of that.'

'You mean I can't touch you?'

'I didn't mean that. It's just that it's early days.'

'What about your letters?' I said.

She kicked at a tuft of grass and hung her head. 'What about them?'

'You keep on telling me how much you love me.'

Her face turned scarlet again. 'That's what folk say in letters. Everyone says it.'

'Don't you mean it?'

She shook her head from side to side, not in denial but in exasperation at my question. 'It's just how folk talk.'

'I wanted to say thank you,' I said.

'What for?'

'All those fags.'

'That's all right,' she said. 'Don't mention it.'

'It's very good of you.'

Her head jerked up. 'Why do you always talk so posh? It sounds daft.'

'I'm sorry,' I said. 'I didn't know it sounded posh.'

'Well it does.' She kicked harder at the tuft of grass and finally dislodged it. 'We should be getting back. Not together. They'll be watching out for us.'

'We've only just got here,' I said.

'It wasn't my idea' said Doris. 'You were the one who wanted to come.' She dug her fists into the pockets of her raincoat and looked around her with distaste. 'Empty fields and a lot of cow muck. What did you want to come here for?'

'Just to talk to you.'

'You've done that.'

'Not really,' I said. 'We've not talked at all.'

She shrugged her shoulders. 'There's not a lot to say.'

It was what I had decided long before, but I was reluctant to concede defeat. 'Do you like my letters?'

'They're all right. You use a lot of funny words.'

'What do you mean? Which words?'

'I don't know.' She tossed her hair and adjusted the slide. 'You said something about music being the food of love and what sort of songs did I like. I didn't know what you were getting at.'

'It's from a play. Shakespeare.'

'Oh, him. What did you want to bring him into it for?'

'It just seemed appropriate.'

She stamped her foot. 'You see what I mean? Appropriate! No one round here says things like that.'

I grabbed her shoulders and kissed her. Her lips were parted and our teeth clashed. It was quite painful and I let her go immediately. She backed away, scrubbing her mouth with the sleeve of her raincoat. The colour had entirely left her face and I realised that she was scared. 'It's all right,' I said. 'I'm not going to hurt you.'

'I'll scream if you touch me,' said Doris. 'Just you keep off.'

As she backed away one leg was lassooed by a bramble and she fell into a low tangle of bushes. Thorns bloodied her hands as she pulled herself free. I did not move. It seemed safer to stay where I was. I desperately did not want her to scream. At length she stood up and dusted herself down.

'I expect you're proud of yourself,' she said. 'Upsetting me like that.'

'No I'm not. I just wanted to talk to you.'

'You call that talking?'

'Sort of,' I said.

'It may be what your sort call talking,' said Doris. 'I'd call it something else.'

She performed a smart, almost military about-turn and marched off down the track towards the main road and the school. That was the end of that, I thought. No more letters, which was good, and no more cigarettes, which was bad. I began to prepare my excuses to Harry Barnes.

He was not pleased. 'You've buggered it up now,' he said.

'Hard cheese.'

'You could say you're sorry.'

'Why should I?'

'You've let us all down,' said Harry. 'She was a generous lass, was Doris. She did well by you.'

'Just hang on,' I said 'You'll find someone else.'

He sighed dramatically. 'There's not many like her. D'you think you could talk her round?'

'I doubt it.'

'Pity she doesn't fancy me,' he said.

'Shall I write you a reference?'

'The day I have to ask you for something like that I'll cut my throat,' said Harry. He was not far from being offended, I realised. He did not have a regular girl friend and he did not like the fact being mentioned however indirectly. He did not lack boldness, however, and it was with him that I met the town girls in Darwen. Several of them used to gather outside a chip shop on the way to the station and Harry nudged my elbow as we drew near.

'They're not like Doris, this lot.'

'How do you mean.'

He flipped his right hand up and down and blew on his fingers. 'They're hot stuff.'

I looked ahead with fresh interest. 'Honestly?'

'Scout's honour,' said Harry.

We slowed our pace as we approached the shop and two girls detached themselves from the group and sauntered towards us. 'You're from the Homes,' said one with streaky blond hair.

'What if we are?' said Harry.

'Nothing, we just wondered. What's it like there?'

'Bloody awful,' said Harry.

'Do they beat you?'

'Something rotten.'

'What for?'

'Going after girls,' said Harry.

'They never!'

'Yes they do,' I said.

We walked on towards the station. There was a short-cut down a row of derelict buildings on which the doors hung tipsily and through whose windows you could see flowered wallpaper, dropsical with damp, and grates on which rust had gnawed through the blacklead. The girls giggled behind us.

'Don't tell them your proper name,' hissed Harry.

'Why not?'

'I'm Dave and you're Terry.' He stopped and leaned against the wall. 'Are you following us?' he enquired.

'It's a free country,' said the blond girl. Her hands were deep in her overcoat pockets and she moved her arms stiffly so that the coat swung open like double doors to reveal a button-through dress.

The other girl was dark and wore a green cape fastened at the neck with a bone toggle. 'We've seen you go by before,' she said.

'You'll know us next time then,' said Harry.

The dark girl motioned towards the next house on the left. 'We used to live there. They moved us out to the new estate.' She pointed to an upstairs window. 'That was my bedroom.'

'Show it to us then,' said Harry. 'I've never seen a lass's bedroom.'

The dark girl shook her head. 'I don't trust you. You look wicked. But I'll show him.' She pinched my arm gently. 'I can trust you, can't I?'

I nodded dumbly, my heart jumping in my throat. The blonde took Harry's hand. 'Don't feel left out,' she said. 'I've got something to show you.'

He put his arm round her waist. 'Can I guess what it is?'

'If you like.'

'Does it whistle?'

'No.'

Does it have hair on it?'

'No.'

'Does it have milk in it?'

She giggled and tugged away from him. 'Sometimes.'

'I've got it,' said Harry. 'A bald coconut.'

'Daft thing,' said the blonde. 'What's your name?'

'He's Terry and I'm Dave,' said Harry. 'What's yours?'

The two girls exchanged swift glances. 'I'm Doreen,' said the dark girl. 'She's Fiona. Posh, isn't it?'

For several seconds we all savoured our pseudonyms. It was like putting on a cloak which made the wearer invisible. My heart still hammered in my chest but I breathed deeply and hoped that my voice would sound normal. 'Show me your house then.'

Doreen took my hand and led me through the gaping door. She propped it shut and then, with her back to it, locked both arms around my neck and pulled my face down to hers. I felt her tongue squirm into my mouth and tasted, very faintly, the chips she had been eating. I forgot to breathe and stumbling on the broken floor reached out and felt her, soft and pliant beneath the cape.

She held me at arm's length. 'Don't undo any buttons,' she said.

'I wasn't going to.'

She put her head to one side and looked at me carefully. 'No,' she said. 'I don't suppose you were.'

I bent forward to kiss her again but she put her finger to my lips. 'Don't open your mouth so wide,' she said. 'Half open like this and keep your lips soft.' She tilted her face and our mouths met and melted together. The difference was amazing. I kept my left arm around her neck and with my right hand squeezed her right breast. She pressed her body against me and I thrust my right thigh between her legs. She let it remain there for a count of five, then stepped back. I tried to jam her against the door but she slipped to one side.

'You're a fast learner,' she said.

'Too fast?'

'Fast enough.'

It had been like an exercise, I thought; a routine followed by numbers. We went through the motions again and I tried to replace my thigh with my right hand but she evaded me. I was conscious of having made a wrong move.

'We've only just clicked,' she said.

'That doesn't matter.'

'Yes it does. You think I'm easy.'

'No I don't,' I lied.

'I know you do. You're wrong though.' She patted her hair and straightened her cape. 'Fiona,' she called. 'We're going.'

I pushed the door open and we walked down the alley. 'Did you really live here?' I asked.

'Till I was eleven. It was better than where we are now.'

'Why's that?'

'It's boring. Inside lavs and all that, but boring.'

'Shall we see each other again?'

'If you like.'

We waited for Harry and Fiona, then both girls walked back along the alley and Harry and I continued to the station. We jumped on the train just as it was pulling out ('Mind that bloody door,' bawled a guard) and as we cleared the town Harry jabbed his right hand under my nose. 'Smell that,' he ordered.

A musty, meaty odour clung to his fingers. 'First time,' he said. 'No messing about. Straight up and away.' He leaned back and watched the telephone poles whizz by. 'How did you get on?'

'Pretty fair.'

'Did she let you?'

'Let me what?'

'You know.' He grabbed my hand and sniffed the fingers. 'I thought not,' he said.

'She said we'd only just clicked.'

'She didn't mean you to take any notice. She'd have let you.'

'I don't think she's like that.'

'They're all like that.' said Harry. He put his feet on the seat opposite and polished the toe-caps on the dusty moquette. 'It was smashing,' he said. 'Next time I'll do her properly.'

'Where?'

'In the house. Against the wall.'

It was as if he had shown me a snapshot: the girl with her dress unbuttoned, her shoulders braced against the flowered wallpaper, her legs apart and her pelvis (what colour was her hair? I wondered) butting against Harry. 'You'll get caught,' I said.

'It'd be worth it.'

He was right, I thought. 'Do you like her?' I asked.

'She's all right.'

'What did you talk about?'

He cupped his hands about his face and breathed deeply. 'Nothing,' he said.

'You must have said something.'

Harry shook his head. 'Not Fiona and me. Straight at it. No messing about.' He smiled to himself reminiscently. 'Some blokes make a living at it. Just think of that.' Green leaves and blossom skidded by the carriage window but Harry was seeing other things. I could almost read his mind. He was imagining a land of counterpane in which he joyously bucked and heaved without constraint. It was always warm. There was the best of company. There was no one to tell him to behave or stop. He exhaled softly and stretched himself until his joints cracked. 'Just imagine,' he said.

Sadie had her suspicions that I was seeing other girls. 'You don't care about me any more,' she said.

'Don't be daft,' I said. 'Of course I do.'

'We're just stuck here doing the same old thing. It's the same every day. You think it's boring.'

'Never,' I said. But she was right. It had not occured to me before, but Sadie had put her finger on what blighted most relationships at the Homes. They were not allowed to develop. Lives were circumscribed by convention and necessity. Needs were met but never indulged. Rules were unbending. To survive, to convince one's self that there was a future beyond the world of Mr Buller and Sister Beryl, it was imperative to disobey.

'It'll be different when we're in London,' said Sadie. It was a phrase she used often, both as a threat and a promise. The promise was that one day we would be together, away from the constraints of the Homes. Everything would be different then. We would do as we liked. The threat was that unless we remained faithful to each other throughout the testing time, there would be no reward, no shared tomorrow in which all mysteries would be revealed. In London everything was possible. It was an article of faith to which we both clung. But it was very distant at times; especially when there seemed to be consolation closer to hand.

'You've got another girl,' said Sadie. 'I can tell.'

'Not like you,' I said truthfully.

'What does that mean?'

'There's no one steady. No one that counts.'

'You've been out with someone though.'

'Not what you'd call going out.'

She clicked her tongue in exasperation. 'Stop trying to be clever.'

'I'm not. Honestly.'

'You don't know what honest means.' Her voice was sharpening in the way I remembered, as though each vowel was being stropped somewhere behind her nose before being released.

'Oh well,' I said. 'If you don't believe me . . .'

'How can I believe you?'

'What chances have I got of going out with anyone? Just think.'

'You go and stay with that friend.'

'He's got no time for girls,' I said. 'We go out shooting. And we saw the wrestling at Blackburn Baths.'

Sadie sniffed suspiciously. She was wearing a blouse which had a lace collar and small lace panels over each breast. She saw me looking and tugged her cardigan across the gap. 'You must think I'm stupid,' she said.

'Why's that?'

'What the eye doesn't see the heart doesn't grieve for. That's what you think.'

'I don't know what you're talking about.'

'Yes you do. Out of sight, out of mind.'

'Talk sense,' I said. Sometimes with Sadie I felt I was being addressed in code and it was becoming too much trouble to sift out the meaning. I touched her hair but she shied away. I wanted to explain to her that needs and loyalties were not necessarily linked and that I was not betraying her by seeing other girls, but the argument was beyond any logic that I could muster. My tongue felt too big for my mouth and I could not speak the words.

She smoothed back the hair I had touched as if cancelling out the imprint of my hand. 'People have feelings,' she said.

'I know they do.'

'If you want to break it off all you need to do is say so.'

I shook my head. 'I don't want to break it off.'

'Well then,' said Sadie.

'Well what?'

'We'd better try again,' she said.

I put my hand to her face and she did not pull away. I felt the warmth of her flesh and when she moved against me I forgot her petulance and her pinched vowels and her way of looking down her nose and was aware only of her presence like someone in a dark house whose company, although not sovereign, banished at least some of the ghosts. Perhaps I did the same for her. I traced the line of her lips with my fingertip and gasped when she nipped it between her teeth. 'Just as you like,' I said. 'We'd be daft to break it off now.'

Seven

WE WERE HAY-MAKING when I first heard the rumour that Mr Buller was leaving. It was early summer. The mornings were fresh and the swallows were still building their nests beneath the eaves of the barn, but it had been unusually fine throughout May and by the second week of June the grass looked scorched at the tip and rustled like paper when the wind stirred it. There were four meadows to be cut. All of them were on an incline, tilted like yellow rugs towards the moors· They were bounded by drystone walls which we repaired each year, filling in the core with rubble and fitting chunks of rock in the gaps like pieces in a jigsaw. The meadows were perfectly square, as if they had been measured out with a pencil and ruler. They were not playgrounds but part of a working farm and the uncut grass was somehow frivolous and contrary to the natural order. Turning it into hay restored discipline.

The first cut was made on Saturday morning. Mr King made a circuit of the meadow in the red farm tractor and from the road it looked as though a thin rind had been peeled away from the perimeter, outlining and emphasising the job to be done. By midday the meadow was half cut. Grass lay in dusty swathes. Swallows dipped low for insects and rabbits occasionally bolted from the standing grass in the centre.

The farmer had already shot half a dozen. He would allow no one else to handle his gun, but gave us his empty cartridge cases, still warm and smelling of gunpowder. His name was Mr Jackson. He lived with his wife in a cottage by the farm and boasted that no one outside the family circle had ever set foot over his doorstep. 'It's private,' he said. 'I want no one looking in on me.'

'You mean lads,' said Doss, who had recently left school and joined the farm as a labourer.

'I mean anyone,' said Mr Jackson. 'Lads or Labour Masters, it makes no difference. I kept the governor standing in the rain one day. Right peeved he was. But, like I told him, a man's home is his castle. He had no answer to that.' He smiled at the memory. 'Anyhow,' he said, 'He'll be off soon. He can knock at other folks' doors.'

'Off where?' I asked.

Mr Jackson loaded his gun and thumbed the safety catch. 'He's got himself promoted. Another branch somewhere, a lot grander than this.' He handed me his string of rabbits, already paunched and beaded with flies. 'Take these back to the farm and tell them we're ready for raking. Don't take all day. And don't forget to come back yourself. There's plenty to do.'

Mr Jackson was renowned for his independence. He managed the farm for the Homes but neither sought nor accepted advice on how it should be run. It was difficult to guess his age; most likely he was in his late forties. But he did not gossip about his past experiences, he had no friends on the staff in whom he confided, so there was no way of assessing what he had been or what he had done before coming to us. His face and arms were deeply tanned and in all weathers and all seasons he wore a flat cap, stiff with grease. He made small, grim jokes about how little he was paid and how much the farm was expected to produce, but he never actually complained, and whatever the job, he was the first to arrive and the last to leave. He seemed to take pleasure in giving more than was legitimately expected, so that however curt his manner, however arrogantly he behaved, no one could criticise him or suggest that he acted differently.

I gave the rabbits to his wife, a small fair woman who came to the door wearing a green overall. Over her shoulder I could see the end of a table covered with a chenille cloth and a piano with brass candlesticks. There was a smell of fried onions and a whiff of bleach which suggested that she had been washing clothes. But they were clues which I was unable to pursue. Mrs Jackson opened the door a bare six inches and took the rabbits from my hand. 'Right you are then,' she said and closed it in my face. I could imagine how frustrated Mr Buller had been.

As we raked the meadow all that afternoon the rumour of his going passed down the lines of hay-makers. There were fifteen to the line, each of us clasping an ash rake with which we combed the grass into a long, floppy roll to dry in the sun. The stubble pierced our plimsolls and the rakes blistered our hands. I was drunk on the scent of grass, drugged by the pleasant monotony of the job.

'D'you reckon it's true about Buller?' asked Doss.

'I don't see why not.'

'Where's he going?'

'Christ knows. Who cares?'

'Who d'you think's coming here?'

'Why don't you ask him?'

'I might at that.' He leaned on his rake and watched the tractor circling the last stand of grass. In the heat of the afternoon the noise of its engine was reduced to a dull roar, like a bee trapped beneath a tumbler. I saw a rabbit break from cover and Mr Jackson's dog, a black and white lurcher, streak after it and catch it before it reached the edge of the meadow. It was already dead by the time we heard it scream.

Next day Mr Buller took us to morning service while Mr King mowed the second meadow. As we marched up the hill from the village we could see the tractor crawling towards us, leaving a fresh pleat of grass in its wake. The pattern was pleasing. The hay-making was going according to plan.

'By the sweat of thy brow shalt thou earn thy bread,' said Mr Buller, walking behind me.

'Beg pardon, sir.'

'From the Bible. Look it up.'

His tone was jovial. He wore a light summer suit and swung his walking stick so that it hummed in the air.

'Ready for work this afternoon?' he enquired.

'We don't mind, sir.'

'I should think not. Sunshine, fresh air, a job worth doing.' He looked heavenwards and spread his arms as if asking the Lord's approval. 'I'd be with you myself if I wasn't so busy,' he said. 'We must all do our bit. Remember that.'

Normally we spent Sundays at chapel, or reading books, or walking sedately. But with hay-making the rules were altered. Bringing in the hay was always a race against the weather and everyone who could hold a rake or load a cart was conscripted while the sun shone. The fundamentalists grumbled. Sunday, they said, was the day of rest. But they were overruled and the hay-making went on. Mr Buller's offer of help, uttered and instantly withdrawn, was not to be taken seriously. He supported many things in theory – the war effort, the ATC, missionaries, prison reform. The list was endless and always being added to when some news item or popular appeal caught his fancy. But in practice he did very little. In his imagination the word instantly became the deed. To suggest that he promised more than he delivered would have been offensive. Mr Buller lived in a glitter of good intentions, not perceiving that they were rarely fulfilled.

He sang the refrain of 'All Things Bright and Beautiful', one of the morning's hymns, and adjusted the rose in his lapel. 'Exquisite scent,' he murmured.

'Is it true you're leaving, sir?' asked Doss.

Mr Buller did not even break step. 'Where did you hear that?'

'They're all talking about it, sir.'

Mr Buller smiled and sighed. 'Are they indeed.' He marched on in silence.

'But is it true, sir?' I persisted.

He kept his eyes on the tractor, now cutting diagonally across the meadow. The slope was so steep that it seemed to move like a fly, glued to the ground by its slowly turning wheels. 'We all move on,' he said at last. 'Nothing stands still.' He pointed ahead with his stick. 'Slow but sure brings harvest home.'

I did not remark on the quotation in case he told me to look it up. 'But does that mean you're going, sir?'

'Going?' he said, as if testing the word for air-worthiness. 'Yes, I am. Next month, as a matter of fact. I've been asked to take over another branch. In the south. Very different from here. Closer to home for Mrs Buller. Her parents are getting on a bit. She feels she ought to be near them.' He did not sound entirely convincing and I realised that what I was hearing was an early rehearsal of the announcement which would later become official.

'Good luck, sir,' said Doss.

Mr Buller bobbed his head. 'That's kind of you. We all need luck, some of us more than others.' He threw back his head and laughed. Already he sounded more sure of himself.

'Who'll be coming here, sir?' asked Doss.

'No one you know. He's called Mr Rome. A remarkable man, I'm told. Progressive, just as I hope I'm progressive. But different.' He dug me in the ribs. 'Remember the saying: When in Rome, do as the Romans do. Bear it in mind. It could save you a lot of trouble. And, for the time being, keep all this to yourselves.'

He did not, of course, expect us to. He had been aware of the rumours circulating and seized the opportunity to prepare the ground for the statement he would eventually make. Mr Buller was excited by his own good news and found difficulty in keeping it to himself. That was why he had answered our questions. He liked to be the centre of attention. To know that people were talking about him was a tonic. He smartened his pace and sang more loudly. 'Close ranks up there,' he called. 'Swing your arms as you go through the branch. Show a bit of swank.'

As we passed Argyle house I saw Sadie hanging out of a bedroom window. She blew me a kiss which was intercepted by Mr Buller who smiled even more merrily than before. 'Love's young dream,' he said.

I could not think how to respond. Roguishness was new to Mr Buller. It was an end-of-term feeling inspired by his leaving, I decided, but I could do no more than grin sheepishly. The good humour might dissolve at any moment and it was safer to say nothing.

That afternoon I worked beside Harry Barnes. We raked the hay in the first meadow into cocks, loose domes of fragrant grass spangled with clover and trefoil, ready to load on to the cart. It was drawn by Major, Captain's successor, a sweet-tempered shire horse whose only fault was to stand implacably on the foot of whoever was leading him. With sweat clogging his coat and flies clustering in the corners of his eyes, he would plant his great polished hoof on the plimsoll standing beside him and wait patiently, deaf to all exhortations, until he felt the shafts of the cart bear down on his harness, the signal that it was time to move on.

'Don't pull on his bit like that,' said Mr Jackson when I tried to haul Major forward. 'Tell him what you want. He's not daft.' He took hold of the hair which draped Major's fetlock and lifted it gently. 'Move it,' he said, clicking his tongue, and Major shifted his weight.

I hopped on one foot until I fell over, then lay on the stubble inspecting my bruises. 'I think he's broken it,' I said.

Mr Jackson stroked Major's pink nose. 'Not him. He's a good old boy. You can ride him to the barn if you like.'

'Can we take turns?' asked Harry.

'You can ride him coming back.' Mr Jackson folded a sack as a makeshift saddle and helped me to mount. 'He'd split you in two without that. He's got a back like a chapel roof.'

Even with the sack to protect me Major's spine sliced painfully into my crotch. Plodding along the road each step that he took was like a blow from a blunt chisel. I winced in anticipation as Harry urged him into a slow trot, but I remained where I was. I felt like a knight riding into battle. The world was far below. Passers-by were serfs and vagabonds. I wished that I had a helmet to wear and a lance to carry. I wished that Sadie could see me. 'Love's young dream,' Mr Buller had said and I imagined myself as some lady's champion, sporting her favour, questing in her name. It was a fantasy I could never describe to Harry. It had nothing to do with him or Fiona or Doreen. It was private; a story to tell myself. We slithered to a halt beside the barn and I lowered myself to the ground.

'Have you still got your tackle?' asked Harry.

'More or less.'

'They say that riding horses makes women randy.'

'How's that?'

He rocked himself backwards and forwards. 'Use your imagination. That's what they do.'

'You've been reading books,' I said.

'No I've not. Fiona told me.'

'She's got a dirty mind.'

'I'm happy to say.' He grasped Major's bridle and led him beneath the circular window of the loft. 'Are you ready up there?' he called.

Ray Clutton and a boy named Bristow looked out. 'We've been ready for ages,' said Ray. 'Let's get cracking.'

Forking the hay into the loft was done in three stages. Harry and I heaved it up from the cart, Ray threw it back from the window and Bristow stacked it against the far wall. It was the worst job of the three. The air was full of dust and fragments of hay and the ambition of the others was to go so fast that the end of the line was overwhelmed. We knew we had won when we heard a muffled cry, telling us to let up. We paused for a moment and saw Bristow's head emerge from the porthole. 'Silly beggars,' he said. His face was streaked with dirt and his spectacles were opaque.

'Something wrong?' asked Harry.

'I can't breathe.'

'Didn't they teach you? It's easy.' Harry put his hands on his hips and demonstrated the deep breathing exercises we performed at school. For good value he executed several knee-bends, then lay on his back and pedalled his legs in the air.

'Joke over,' said Ray. 'Change places.'

Inside the loft was like being beneath an upturned boat. Massive beams spanned the roof, the bleached timbers soaring upwards into darkness. There was a hush that was like being in church and sparrows cheeped and fluttered against the tiles. The porthole was filled with blue sky, instantly obscured as the hay came tumbling through. I forked it back and thought of nothing. Maintaining the rhythm was all that mattered. Sweat streamed down my face and soaked my shirt. I tried to keep my mouth closed, but the dust blotted my tongue to leather. My shoulders ached and I felt the blisters on my hands burst, one by one. Suddenly it was over. The porthole cleared and the sky shone through.

'We beat the buggers,' said Harry.

'Only just.'

'That's good enough.' He looked around him, as if seeing the place for the first time. 'I'd like to bring Fiona here. Just imagine.' He sank down on the hay, his arms and legs outstretched. 'Just think of it,' he said.

We clambered down the ladder into the farmyard and sluiced off the dust in the drinking trough. Ray combed his hair and pinched his quiff into place. 'It's true about Buller then,' he said.

'That's what he told us.'

'What did he say about this other bloke?'

I tried to recall Mr Buller's description: 'Progressive.'

'Just like him,' said Harry.

'All piss and wind,' said Ray.

We sighed in chorus. There was an official language which we recognised and instinctively distrusted. It meant both more and less than it said. It was used by teachers and office workers and whoever composed the communiqués reporting limited advances and strategic withdrawals that Mr Buller read out in his current-affairs bulletins. It was not designed to tell the truth, but to convey an impression of the truth, like a photograph taken from a dramatic angle.

Sometimes an outright lie was concealed; more often the lie was diluted or tinctured with some other flavour which gave it an artificial glamour or robustness. We could not always tell what we were meant to think. But we were natural sceptics. To doubt was to lessen the risk of being deceived.

We worked until dusk. The loft filled up with hay, gradually closing the eye of the porthole. There was another loft to fill and after that a number of Dutch barns. But with the dew falling and bats flitting overhead we shouldered our rakes and followed the tractor home.

As a treat we were allowed half an hour's swim. The pool, which was covered over in the winter months and used for socials and indoor games, was filled with water from the moors. It was not like the school baths, clear and tasting of chlorine, but brown with peat and silky to the touch. We did not wear costumes and to dive naked into the tawny basin and feel our grime stripped away was like being baptised. We came to the surface breathless and reborn.

I paddled to the deep end and floated on my back. There were raw patches on the palms of both hands and the nails on my right foot were already turning black from being trodden on by Major. I closed my eyes and drifted. If I had been alone I could have gone to sleep. But there was no chance of that. Harry Barnes surfaced behind me and ducked my head under water. I rolled over and grabbed for his cock. Ray Clutton jumped in from the side and dive-bombed us both.

'Race you to the other end,' he shouted.

It was no fun racing Ray because he always won. He could do the American crawl and the side stroke and he already held a life-saving certificate. The previous year he had swum a mile in the Bury Baths and when he was called up he intended to volunteer as a frogman. I trod water and watched him pass and re-pass me, his head swivelling from side to side, his feet churning like propellors, and I hauled myself out and sat on the edge until Mr King told me to get dressed.

'You don't want to catch cold,' he said. 'I've seen men put on a charge for that. Wilful self-neglect. Damaging crown property.'

It was still light when we got outside. Banks of cloud were pressing down from the moor, but to the west the sky was a luminous pink. The swim had refreshed me and I felt wide awake. 'Come for a walk,' said Harry.

'Where to?'

'I'll show you that curlew's nest. It's only ten minutes.'

'You'll never find it now.'

'I've marked the place. I could take you to it blindfold.'

I believed him. Harry was the best bird's-nester I knew. That spring he had shown me a kestrel's nest in the chimney of a derelict mill behind the village. While I waited at the bottom he had climbed the chimney and come down with three eggs in a knotted handkerchief held in his teeth. Then he had climbed up again to put them back. I had never been able to find a curlew's nest myself. 'Just ten minutes,' I said.

We passed Mosscrop House on the far side of the road, then the gardener's cottage and the playing fields. Ahead lay Little Switzerland, a stretch of open country sandwiched between farm land, traversed by small streams and dotted with clumps of trees which clung to the sides of miniature ravines. No crops grew there and it was poor grazing, but it was picturesque. Each winter when the drifts piled high it was photographed by the local paper ('Snow Scenes to Rival the Alps') and featured in a set of picture postcards which were displayed on a rack in the post office.

We climbed the low wall by a strip of corrugated iron that Harry had placed as a marker and splashed through a patch of waterlogged ground to a gate on the far side of the field. A solitary lapwing flew up beneath our feet and trailed its reflection over the broken water. Harry unlatched the gate and hooked it behind us. 'We take a short-cut across here and it's in the next meadow,' he said.

I looked around me uneasily. 'Aren't we near Cobb's place?'

'He'll not be here now,' said Harry.

'Let's hope not.'

Mr Cobb was a farmer who lived with his son in a ramshackle cottage half a mile up the road. He was a widower who was rumoured to have refused to summon a doctor when his wife was dying of pneumonia. His son was an idiot who had attended the branch school until his father claimed him for work on the farm and whom we saw occasionally driving a herd of cows from one scrubby pasture to another, a torn sack shrouding his head and shoulders. Mr King had once found him foraging in the swill bins, a broken loaf in one hand, a kipper skin in the other. 'It was worse than India,' he told us. 'I reckon he was starving.'

Shortly afterwards an NSPCC man was seen heading towards Cobb's farm. There was no prosecution, but Mr Cobb held the Homes reponsible for the intrusion into his private life and we were warned by Mr Buller to stay clear of him and his property. We were on it now, I realised. The short-cut took us across one of his pastures. Beyond it we were in Little Switzerland again, but for several acres we were trespassing.

We had almost reached neutral ground when he stepped from behind a hawthorn. There was a dog beside him, a cross between an Alsatian and a collie, and his son followed at his heels. He studied us for a moment, then crooked a finger. 'Come here.'

'We're just passing through,' said Harry.

Mr Cobb raised his stick slightly, as if it was alive and he was having difficulty in controlling it. 'Come here,' he said again.

We stayed where we were and Mr Cobb's son giggled excitedly. Without looking round, his father lashed out with his stick and hit the boy across the shins. He did not take his eyes from us for one second. 'I told you to come here,' he said. 'If you don't I'll set the dog on you.'

It suddenly seemed much darker than it had been a moment before. A cold wind sneaked down the neck of my shirt and I shivered. 'I'll not tell you again,' said Mr Cobb.

'We're sorry,' I said. 'We didn't know we were on your land.'

'Didn't know? Is that it? I know your sort. Thieves and bloody nosey-parkers. Don't tell me you didn't know.' His stick quivered in his hand and sensing the movement the dog growled in sympathy.

Harry nudged me with his hip. 'Run for it,' he said and darted for the wall. The dog went after him and Mr Cobb came after me. He was wearing gum boots which slowed him down and I was a good ten yards ahead when I tripped over a bramble and plunged to the ground. He was on to me before I could get up. I saw the stick rise and fall and felt an amazing pain across my back. I screamed in surprise as much as in hurt. He hit me again, this time across the face. I curled into a ball and tried to roll away but he followed me, slashing and hacking at my head and body as if trying to dismember it. I lost count of the number of times he hit me; there was no part of me that escaped punishment. As he flailed me with his stick he shouted abuse, one obscenity streaming into the next. He seemed unable to stop and with a curious detachment, as if noting the fact during a lesson at school, I knew that unless I escaped he would kill me.

There was a moment's respite and squinting through my fingers I saw him change his stick from one hand to the other before hitting me again. With a desperate energy I dived at his belly, butting him with my head and bowling him over into a shallow pool where he lay for a second before scrambling to his knees and crawling towards me, the stick still in his hand.

I turned and ran. I felt no pain. I felt nothing but terror. I heard Mr Cobb shouting for me to stop and urging his son to give chase. I heard the dog barking and when I reached the road looked over my shoulder to see it bounding after me. I grabbed a loose brick from the wall and aimed at its head. I missed and threw another. There was a yelp and the dog turned about, limping away on three legs. It was almost completely dark but the soggy ground reflected the last of the sunset, a carpet of rose across which my pursuer still came, his gum boots churning the puddles, his coat flapping about his ankles.

I ran home without stopping. It was like being awake within a nightmare, alert but unable to shed the dream. However hard I ran I knew that he would still follow, not with any real hope of catching me but because his anger would not let him rest. He reminded me of cattle tormented by warble flies, stung by something they could not see and galloping without sense or direction until they were exhausted and stood shaking and flecked with foam while the flies sang on behind them.

I hobbled down the path by the side of the house and let myself in by the back door. In the washroom I looked at myself in the mirror and saw a stranger. One eye was closed, the cheekbone split. My nose was too swollen to breathe through and my shirt was torn. I began to peel it off gingerly and found it was stuck to my back. From my shoulders to my knees my flesh was a bloody lattice. My ribs were criss-crossed with welts and bruises and the knuckles of my right hand were twice their normal size. The inventory of my injuries was endless. I ran a basin of warm water and tried to clean myself up.

Sister Joyce found me when I was half done. 'What on earth's happened to you?' she demanded.

'I had an accident.'

'I can see that.' She dragged a chair from the shower room and pushed me down on it. 'Sit there and let's see what the damage is.' She inspected me like a trainer checking a boxer between rounds. Her fingers pressed and and probed. She felt my ribs and my kidneys. She told me to undress completely and I did not argue. 'Does it hurt there?' she asked and when I shook my head she gave me a towel to wrap round me. 'You're lucky. It could have been worse. I'll do some patching up, then you can tell me what happened.'

I described looking for the curlew's nest and being surprised by the farmer while she dabbed me with antiseptic and witch hazel and Vaseline and taped my knuckles and tied bandages until I felt trussed like a parcel.

'You're in the wrong,' she said. 'You know that. You were trespassing.'

'We didn't do any damage.'

'You're sure? You didn't steal anything?'

'We were just out for a walk,' I said.

'You should have been back here. You've only yourself to blame.'

I did not reply and she tilted my chin with her finger. 'Don't feel so sorry for yourself. Worse things happen at sea. Go and get changed. We'll have to tell Mr Buller.'

'Where's Sister Beryl?'

'Out visiting. It's her night off. I said you were lucky. Go on now, make haste.'

As we crossed the road to the governor's house I saw that Mr Cobb had got there before us. His dog was tethered outside and his son sat on the front step. He pointed his finger at me and giggled. He was tying knots in a piece of string, prising them loose and tying them again. He held it up for us to admire.

'Is that his boy?' asked Sister Joyce.

'He was there too.'

She studied him briefly. 'He looks worse off than you.'

A maid showed us into Mr Buller's study where Mr Cobb sat in a chair by the desk. His cap was on his knees and one hand rested on the crook of his stick.

'That's what he hit me with,' I said.

'Trespassers get what they deserve,' said Mr Cobb. 'And what did you do to my dog? Broke his leg I shouldn't wonder.' He turned to Mr Buller and slapped his hand on the desk top. 'I want paying for that. Proper compensation.'

It was the first time I had seen him close to. His hair was dark and close-cropped. His face was seamed with dirt as if

successive layers of sweat had dried on it. The bridge of his
nose was deeply indented by a pair of steel-rimmed
spectacles and he smelled of paraffin and mildew. 'He
assaulted me too,' he said. 'I should be talking to the police
instead of coming here. I want something done about it.'

Mr Buller stared at Mr Cobb's hand until he put it back in
his lap. 'I'd say you'd already done something,' he said.
'The police might take the same view.' He turned to me.
'And what have you got to say for yourself?'

His tone was not friendly and I understood why. The
smell of roast meat and gravy hung in the air. Mr Buller's
dinner had been interrupted and in a way which he disliked
intensely. The relationship between the Homes and
neighbouring farmers was always difficult. Complaints and
recriminations disrupted goodwill. Mr Buller was on his
way to higher things and he wanted to leave with his
reputation as a diplomat intact. Rancour left a bad after-
taste, whoever created it. As Sister Joyce had already told
me, I was to blame. I did the sensible thing.

'I'm sorry, sir,' I said.

'Understandably.'

'Yes sir,' I said.

'Is anything broken?'

'I don't think so, sir.'

'What on earth were you doing on Mr Cobb's land?'

'Bird's-nesting, sir.'

'And who were you with?'

I had already told Sister Joyce. 'He was with Harry
Barnes,' she said.

'Both grammar-school boys,' said Mr Buller, as if to
himself. 'Setting an example.' He leaned back in his chair. 'I
believe you owe Mr Cobb an apology.'

'He's been badly beaten,' said Sister Joyce. 'I think you
should know that.'

Mr Buller nodded graciously. 'I take it into account.' He
looked at me with raised eyebrows: 'Well?'

'I'm sorry,' I said.

'Is that all?' said Cobb.

'All for now,' said Mr Buller. 'All that concerns this boy. I'm quite sure he won't invade your property again.'

I was being dismissed, but it was not the end of the affair. This performance was for Mr Cobb's benefit. The next time I saw Mr Buller it would be with Harry and there would be no outsider to impress. We would be dressed down, privileges would be revoked, Mr King would be ordered to find us extra work on the Shop. The punishment would not be severe, but it would set an example. At the same time Mr Cobb would be served notice not to take the law into his own hands. Hints would be dropped that charges for assault might have been preferred. His complaints would be carefully noted. Honour would seem to be satisfied.

'Does it hurt?' asked Sister Joyce as we walked home.

'A bit.'

'You can't go to school looking like that. We'll have to send a note tomorrow.'

'What will I do?'

'They're still hay-making, aren't they? Fresh air won't do you any harm.'

In fact, it did me a lot of good. Jokes were made about my black eye and the wicker-work bruises that patterned my legs, but I was found the lightest jobs to do, no one reproached me, and I realised that I had become something of a hero.

'Were you scared?' asked Bristow when we paused for our mid-morning lemonade.

'Scared to death,' I said truthfully. 'So would you have been.'

'Did you faint?'

I shook my head. Fainting was part of the mythology of flogging. We had all read how even the strongest men passed out if the pain was too great to endure. But the comics were wrong. 'I kept trying to think how to get away,' I said. 'I had to stay sharp.'

'Show us your back,' said Bristow.

I unbuttoned my shirt and slowly drew it over my head. I heard a chorus of admiring hisses and let it fall back. When I looked up Mr Jackson was standing over me. 'Did old Cobb do that?'

'With his stick,' I said.

Mr Jackson chewed on a piece of grass. 'Did Mr Buller see it?'

'He knows about it. Sister Joyce told him.'

'And then what?'

'He told me to say I was sorry.'

Mr Jackson spat out the grass. 'Sorry to Cobb?'

'He said I owed him an apology.'

There was a long silence. Two meadows away the tractor started up and behind me Major tossed his head. 'Whoa there!' said Mr Jackson. 'If you stop by the cottage tonight Mrs Jackson'll have something for you,' he told me. He dusted his hands together and tugged his cap down over his eyes. 'All right, let's be having you.'

We cleared the second meadow that evening. I was too sore to swim and as the others strolled towards the pool, their towels looped about their necks, I knocked on the door of the Jacksons' cottage. It opened grudgingly until Mrs Jackson saw who it was calling. Even then she did not open the door wide. 'Come on in,' she said and the moment I had stepped over the sill, closed it behind me.

Mr Jackson sat at the table eating a plate of cold meat and salad. There was something strange about his appearance and I realised it was the first time I had seen him without his cap. The top of his forehead was dead white, contrasting sharply with his weathered face, and I was reminded of a tea caddy from which someone had unscrewed the lid. He gestured to the chair opposite. 'Have a seat.'

Mrs Jackson poured me a cup of tea and set the sugar bowl beside it. 'Do you like cake?' she asked.

'Yes please.'

She pushed a chocolate Swiss roll towards me. 'Help yourself. There's caraway too if you like it.'

They both watched me as I cut a polite slice and Mr

Jackson laughed. 'That's not enough to feed a sparrow.' He took the knife from my hand and cut a double portion. 'Get that down you,' he said.

I looked around me as I ate. Over the fireplace there was a pair of matching wall plates decorated with cornflowers and poppies. There was a tall brass fender and two armchairs upholstered in red plush and beside one of them lay a pair of carpet slippers. On one wall there was the picture of a sailing boat and on the piano, between the candlesticks which I had glimpsed through the door, there was the photograph of a young man in a silver frame. I committed everything to memory. As far as I knew I was the first visitor the Jacksons had ever admitted to their cottage. It was an experience to savour.

I knew that my invitation had something to do with Mr Cobb, but his name was not mentioned. Instead, Mrs Jackson asked me about school. 'Do you like it there?'

'Most of the time,' I said. 'I can't stand maths though.'

I saw them exchange a glance as though I had reminded them of something long forgotten and Mrs Jackson pulled a handkerchief from her sleeve and dabbed at her nose. 'Just like Robert,' she said.

Mr Jackson put mustard on his meat, stroking it into place with his knife. 'I told you.'

'Who's Robert?' I asked.

'He was our lad,' said Mr Jackson. He pointed to the photograph on the piano. 'That's him. He was just seventeen when that was taken. Three days after he'd sat for his Higher School Certificate.'

'And passed it too,' said Mrs Jackson.

I knew that the story was incomplete. 'What happened?'

'He caught diphtheria,' said Mr Jackson. 'He died.'

I looked for tears but there were none. They had cried themselves dry long ago. 'We wanted him to go on to Agricultural College,' said Mrs Jackson. 'He was that good with stock, he'd have done well with it. There were all sorts of openings. In America even. He didn't have to stay in England. He could have gone anywhere he liked. Everyone said so. But then he took ill. They printed the examination results the week he passed on.'

'I'm sorry,' I said. 'Were you working here then?'

Mr Jackson shook his head. 'It's years ago. I had my own place near Kettering. We sold up and moved out. It seemed the best thing.'

I stayed for half an hour. They showed me albums with photographs of Robert riding his pony, Robert at the seaside, Robert on a bicycle, Robert in the school play. 'He was like you,' said Mrs Jackson, putting the album away, 'he couldn't stand maths either.'

When it was time to go Mr Jackson saw me to the door. 'I paid a call on Mr Cobb this afternoon,' he said. 'I thought someone should have a word with him. Off the record, I mean. He was none too pleased to see me, but he gave me a present. For you rather than me.' He reached behind him and brought up a walking stick, snapped into two equal pieces. 'It's not much use,' he said, 'except as a souvenir.'

I took the pieces from him and fitted them together. 'Get on home,' said Mr Jackson. 'They'll be wondering where you've got to.' Over his shoulder the silver frame of the photograph flared in the dusky room. He winked at me slowly and deliberately and then he shut the door.

Eight

MY BRUISES kept me away from school for two weeks. I was not to regard myself as ill, said Mr Buller, but the beating had been severe and I would probably benefit from a spell of working with my hands in the fresh air. So that I would not fall behind in class he set me exercises in French and mathematics and geography and each afternoon marked my papers while I stared through the window of his office, nervously anticipating his groans of exasperation as he scored through my attempts to solve problems in long division or explain how the Mendips were formed.

'What's wrong with you?' he demanded. 'You're not stupid. Don't you see you can't just dazzle in the subjects you're good at. You've got to work at the others too.'

'I know, sir.'

'Then why don't you?'

'I try to, sir.'

'Then you don't try hard enough.' He prowled round me, flipping the pages of my exercise book and grunting to himself. 'Show me your back,' he said at last.

I pulled up my shirt and bent forward. I was growing used to the routine, but the reactions of those who inspected my wounds were amazingly varied. Sadie had cried and kissed me until her mouth had become hot and grabbing. Harry Barnes had apologised for not staying to help me. Sister Beryl had promptly told me to cover up. Mr Buller was more reflective.

'I think they're beginning to fade.'

'It's hard for me to see, sir.'

'Just here at the edges.' He touched me tentatively with one finger, tracing a shape which I could only imagine. 'It's turning yellow. That's a good sign. Glorious technicolor.

Isn't that what it's called.'

'I think so, sir.'

'Rather spectacular at present. We don't want to put you on show though. We'd have to charge admission.'

He laughed at his own joke and I joined in, but I suddenly understood why I was being kept away from school. If they were seen by outsiders my bruises could reflect badly on the Homes and Mr Buller. He did not wish to be known as the man who condoned floggings or, worse still, carried them out. Only weeks away from taking up a new post, he wanted all his works to bear witness to his intelligence and humanity. In my present state I was an advertisement for aggravated assault. 'I think we can give you a few more days off,' he said. 'Take advantage of it. Make good use of the time.'

I took him at his word. In the mornings I worked in the fields and for two or three hours in the afternoon I completed the test papers devised by Mr Buller. At some time during the day, however, I found an excuse to visit the branch offices where Sadie now worked as a typist. After Christmas she would be leaving for London and her imminent departure hung over us like a small, melancholy cloud. The unhappiness, though, was not unpleasant. Each of us saw the other in an altered light. I thought of Sadie finding new diversions, new friends, perhaps lovers. I was not yet jealous but I imagined myself to be and became more demanding, more reckless in my promises. She, in turn, saw me as the one who was left behind, the solitary figure on the station as the train pulled out, who waved goodbye and then turned elsewhere for consolation. The shadow-play excited us unbearably. In the small, cluttered office smelling of cardboard boxes we clung to each other and swore eternal love. The extravagance was a luxury and a solace. It was also a rehearsal in which each was the other's prompt and inspiration.

We became so adept that, almost without missing a beat, we could pick up where we left off the previous day. Space and opportunity were limited. It was only occasionally that we had the office to ourselves. Two other typists worked in an adjacent room and Sadie's cubby-hole contained the store cupboards and an oak desk mounted with an ancient Underwood. We embraced standing up, wedged in a corner between the cupboards. With her back to the wall Sadie had a view of the path leading to the office door. If someone approached she had time to squeak a warning and slide into her chair, while I straightened my hair and tried to suppress the erection that threatened to burst through my trousers.

Sadie affected not to notice it although it was difficult not to acknowledge the lump that dug into her thigh when we kissed. The longer the kiss lasted, the more the evidence of true love. Ray Clutton boasted that he and Gladys Fisher had made one last for three minutes. He had timed it by keeping one eye on his wrist watch, angled behind Gladys' head. He was most likely telling the truth, but I found that after two minutes I had reached the limits of my endurance. My lips turned numb, my jaw developed a chronic ache, while my erection strained against my underpants like a salmon surging against a net. When its presence became impossible to ignore Sadie let one hand fall, as if by accident, moulding it gently until I gasped for breath and broke away, dizzy with lust.

She allowed me to feel her breasts and once, when we managed to commandeer the office for an entire lunch hour, to finger the liquid slit between her legs. She made faint mewing sounds far back in her throat and sagged in my arms as if I had pressed a button which turned her bones to jelly. There was a strange taste to her mouth and her entire body relaxed and seemed to enfold me like a soft, heavy blanket. She fell back against the wall, her face flushed, a strand of hair pasted across her forehead. I could smell the sea. Something had happened. It was like rainfall or the passing of clouds. The weather had broken but I was still parched. She stroked my face and pecked at my lips with tiny kisses like a bird drinking.

'I love you,' said Sadie. 'Don't forget that.'

'I love you.,
'I'll always love you.'
'Me too.'
'I'll be waiting for you.'
'I'll be thinking of you.'

Our exchanges were as formal as prayers. The litany did not vary. We promised to be faithful, constant and caring day after day after day. After a while it became boring. I tried to think of new things to say, but the ritual was there to be observed. There was no escaping it.

'I love you,' I said.

'I'll always love you,' said Sadie.

My bruises went from black to purple to orange and yellow and at last Mr Buller decided that the drama of my appearance had subsided sufficiently for me to return to school.

'And about time,' said Sister Beryl.

'It's not me that wanted to stay at home.'

'It's not been much of a hardship,' she said. 'Some of us have got eyes. We can see what's going on.'

'What do you mean?'

'You know what I mean. You and that Sadie Bryant. It's a good job she'll be leaving soon.'

'I don't know what you're talking about.'

'You know all right.' She nodded balefully, her lower lip as wet as a peeled plum. 'We can do without that sort of thing, thank you very much.'

I remembered that from Sister Beryl's bedroom there was an unobstructed view of the office window and my heart skipped with rage. 'You mean you've been spying on me.'

'Don't you talk to me like that. We're responsible for you, whether you like it or not. Don't you forget it.'

'I'm not likely to.' I wondered how much she had seen. The distance was too great for her to have discerned any details, but there was little doubt that she had witnessed my comings and goings at times when she knew the office was supposed to be empty. I wanted to tell her it was none of her business, that she had a dirty mind, that love – whatever its degree – was beyond her understanding. But to have done so would have been to recognise her authority, even by denying it. It was better to say nothing. Secrets had their own power and they grew in strength the longer they were kept. It was like belonging to an underground army whose arsenal multiplied behind locked doors. To refer to it was to risk confiscation. I thought of the poster on Darwen railway station showing a smartly dressed woman at a cocktail party surrounded by men in uniform. The slogan read 'Careless talk costs lives'. Sister Beryl was just as dangerous. Her tactic was to provoke reprisals and invite indiscretions. To defeat her all one had to do was remain silent.

'There's no need to look sullen,' she said, trying for the last time. But the moment had passed. I tried to imitate Ray's blinding smile and gathered my school books together. It was a relief to be going back.

On my first day Phil Watson took me home for tea. 'You must come and stay again,' said his mother as she passed round the potted meat sandwiches.

'They won't let me for a while.'

'Why's that?'

'There's been a bit of bother,' I said. 'I got caught trespassing. They've stopped all my privileges.'

'It's not fair,' said Phil. 'He got knocked about too. They're caning him twice over.'

Mrs Watson poured the tea and shot him a glance that would have sliced cheese. 'You speak of what you know.'

'It's true,' I said. 'More or less. It won't last though. We're getting a new governor and he'll make his own rules.'

Mrs Watson tightened her lips. 'About time, it strikes me.' She reached behind her into the drawer of the sideboard. 'I had a letter from your mother. She says it's over a year since she's seen you.'

'I expect she's right.'

'Won't they let you visit her on holiday?'

'It's not usual.'

'You've not got a usual mother. She's an invalid for a start. Don't they know that? Have they got any idea what it's like to lie between four walls, day in, day out? I've a good mind to write to your governor.'

I must have looked alarmed because she covered my hand with her own and squeezed it. 'I only want to do what's best. She worries about you. All the time. I can hardly bear to read her letters. I know just how she feels.'

I seethed inwardly. When I told my mother of my first visit to the Watsons she had asked me for their address so that she could write and thank them for their kindness, one mother to another. It had been a mistake, I could see that now. My mother was incapable of writing a simple thank-you letter. Always, she strove to create a special relationship in which she solicited pity without seeming to. She was stubborn and brave and her complaints always appeared to be forced through gritted teeth. For every favour bestowed she made sure that a favour was returned. She did not wish to be in debt to anyone. I knew that she had sent Mrs Watson a box of handkerchiefs and Phil a silver-plated propelling pencil, gifts which had embarrassed them both.

I could not blame her. Every member of my family tried to get upsides of the others by sending unexpected and unsolicited gifts. They were not extravagant – a pot of marmalade perhaps, or a box of Huntley & Palmer biscuits. But they were tokens of thoughtfulness and generosity which the recipient had to match or acknowledge defeat. My mother's trump card was that she was ill and housebound. Despite her pain she still thought of others. Her friends and correspondents admired her fortitude, then clamoured to be of service.

I was not sure how carefully she calculated the effect of her letters; perhaps not at all. Her instinct, though, did not let her down. Her appeal to the headmaster at the Bluecoat school, when I had not written home for several weeks, inspired him to dress me down publicly at morning assembly. Now it was clear she had been working on Mrs Watson, enlisting her as an ally in some campaign, the details of which I did not yet know.

'If I did write to your governor I'd be very careful what I said,' Mrs Watson continued, after a decent interval.

'What would you write to him about?'

'I'd tell him your mother wants to see you. Needs to see you. I'll pay your fare if that's what they're worried about.'

'Don't say that!' I almost shouted the words and Phil upset his tea in the saucer.

'Please don't say that,' I said more calmly. 'It's not a question of money. It's just that most of the other boys don't have parents to go to. I'm different enough as it is, going out to school and having friends like you. But going away for holidays just doesn't happen.'

'Then it should,' said Mrs Watson.

It was no good, I realised. She had caught the family habit. I was about to be punished by kindness. She had no idea what the consequences would be – digs about privilege from Sister Beryl, resentment on the part of my friends, ill-feeling all round. I was not above plotting for advantage, or scheming for extra perks. But this was too much. I could not avoid the charity, especially as it was for my mother's benefit as much as mine. But possibly I could lessen its impact. 'Don't offer to pay my fare,' I begged.

Mrs Watson drained her cup and dabbed her lips with one of my mother's handkerchiefs. 'If you really don't want me to.'

'I don't. Honestly·'

'Very well then.' She made the rounds with the sandwiches once more. 'But just you remember, your mother's a wonderul woman. You should be proud of her.'

My appetite had vanished. I could eat no more, but I was given a waxed-paper packet of sandwiches to take away with me. 'You can have them for your supper,' said Mrs Watson.

She had no idea what it was like, I thought. She reminded me of those wives and mothers I had read about who sent their men-folk back to the trenches in the First World War with hand-embroidered slippers and smoking jackets: the comforts of home which, if the truth were known, could only be relished at home. Outside it they were a painful reminder of all that was gone.

I threw away the sandwiches as the train hammered into the first tunnel. I could not close the window to the very top and when we came out the other side the carriage was full of smoke. I did not mind. I liked the pungent, back-of-the-fire smell which always touched me with the sad excitement of going places. Journeys by train were never a pure delight or an undiluted misery. Long or short, they created the same mixed feelings. If the journey was a return to school I could always remind myself that when term came to an end I would be travelling home by the same route. And if I was going home I was never forgetful that on the way back I would pass the same houses, the same streams, the same signal boxes. One day a train would take me away from the Homes; but it would be years yet. I tried not to think how long.

Walking from the station I passed field after field which had been cropped of its hay. The new grass was already growing through the stubble, a vivid green which looked too bright to be real. Ahead of me the moors were purple. The heather was in bloom and when I took a deep breath I could taste it on my tongue as if I had licked the honey spoon. It was beautiful, I thought. But the sheep which grazed the stony pastures did not know it, nor did the farmers who tended them. My mother was always writing to me admiringly about nature, investing it with the same sterling qualities she detected in brown bread, spring water and plain cooking. Nature was good in itself. There was no need to explain or understand it. Not that she had any first-hand experience. She had always lived in a house in the Potteries, but she was a romantic whose view of the world was incorrigibly hopeful. She enthused over prospects and vistas. She trusted advertisements and sometimes applauded sermons on the wireless. She held that virtue was its own reward and believed that duty was a prime virtue. She wept when Edward VII abdicated to marry Mrs Simpson, but she was unforgiving. He had betrayed his country, she said. We were lucky to have found out in time.

Part of me wanted to see her again but I was still resentful at the way she had dispatched me to the Homes, finalising the arrangements before I had a chance to protest. I had learned to look after myself since then. I disliked the feeling that – again without my being told – pressures were being exerted, friends manipulated. Already, by implication, I was being advised where my duty lay. I was being shown what was expected of me. Plans were being made and all I had to do was fall in with them.

There were faces at the bedroom windows as I passed Argyle House, but Sadie's was not among them. My mother would not like her, I thought. She would note the faults to which I had become accustomed – the thin voice, the whinnying laugh, the unintentionally haughty look – and she would add to the score. Big breasts were on my mother's black list because she considered them to be vulgar. So was the way in which Sadie walked, swinging her haunches so that her thighs shuddered slightly with each step. My mother would see her as a threat. I resolved to say nothing about her. It was one more secret to keep.

I knew that Mrs Watson would write to the governor as she had intimated, but I hoped that I had managed to put her off for a while. Mr Buller was leaving the branch in four weeks' time. His successor, I surmised, would be too busy settling in to pay attention to me. But I was mistaken. The day before his departure I saw Mr Buller leaving his house with a thin, grey-haired man to whom he was talking vivaciously, waving his arms as though he was conducting an unseen orchestra.

He beckoned me over. 'And this is Philip Oakes,' he said. 'You'll remember we were discussing him.'

The grey-haired man looked me up and down. 'He looks

older than fourteen.'

'Fourteen and a half, sir.'

'And a half,' he added. 'I beg your pardon.'

'This is the new governor,' said Mr Buller. 'Remember your manners.'

We shook hands. 'Pleased to meet you, sir.'

'I hope we shall both be pleased,' he said gravely. 'I understand you've been in a spot of bother.'

'All over now, sir.'

'You feel that, do you? A new start, is it?'

'Yes sir.' His manner confused me. I could not decide whether he was making fun of me with questions which were poised on the brink of irony, or whether he was wholly serious. His next remark decided me.

'I like to see a sense of responsibility.'

'Yes sir,' I said. Mr Rome was evidently not in the business of making jokes. He was not waggish like Mr Buller or a yarn-spinner like Mr King. His comments accumulated weight like beads of water which gathered on a dripping tap and dropped in sober procession.

'You must come and see me,' he said. 'We have things to discuss.'

Mr Buller took his arm. 'When you've settled in.' He led him away, his pink hands again coaxing music from imaginary strings while Mr Rome's grey head nodded in time.

There was a brief ceremony the next morning when Sister Marion presented Mr Buller with a travelling clock and Mr King, on behalf of the rest of the staff, wished him luck. We sang 'To Be a Pilgrim', Mr Buller's favourite hymn. He introduced Mr Rome who said he was glad to be with us and then we all filed out. There was a sense of anticlimax.

'Hardly worth coming,' said Ray as we walked back to the house.

'It got us off a bit of work at any rate.'

'There's that,' he agreed, 'but there's the rest of the day.'

Hay-making was over until the second crop was ready for cutting. On most Saturdays we worked on the Shop until noon, then after lunch and depending on the season we played cricket or football or practised athletics. But the sky was curdled and there was rain in the wind. It was a day for staying indoors.

Sister Beryl, however, had other plans. 'I've a job for you bigger lads,' she announced. 'I want those privies whitewashed.'

There was a general groan. 'That's not fair,' said Skelly. 'It's our afternoon off.'

'It's a Shop job,' said Ray.

Sister Beryl pulled her skirt tight against the fire she had lit when the weather turned. 'The Shop did nothing this morning. It's not my fault Mr Buller's going and we had an extra assembly. The job needs doing and I want you to do it. You can mix the whitewash in the yard. And don't forget to wear your working clothes.' She counted heads across the room. 'There's five of you. It shouldn't take you long. Raymond Clutton, you're in charge.'

We slouched across the yard, our hands deep in our pockets, to see what had to be done. My hidey-hole in the third privy along was empty. I had noticed Sister Beryl watching me one day when I went to make a deposit and as a precaution removed everything I had hidden there. It was a wise move. The next time I inspected the loose brick I saw that it was several degrees out of place and there was a fresh smear of dust on the wall. I had already found somewhere else. There was a flagstone in the furnace room which could be prised up and beneath it I had dug a trench deep enough to take the toffee tin in which I kept my money and a packet of Park Drive. The privies no longer mattered.

'Stinking hole,' said Skelly. He kicked the wall and a shower of rotten whitewash cascaded down.

'It's all got to come off,' said Ray. 'We'll have to scrape it clean before we put the new whitewash on. It won't stick otherwise.'

Spiff picked at his sunburn. 'Who does what then?'

'You scrape,' said Ray. 'You and Skelly and Doss. We'll do the mixing.' He led me away to fill buckets at the tap by the back door and pour them, one by one, into a mixing drum while he stirred the whitewash with a broom handle. It looked like skimmed milk and had a sharp, cool smell. 'Watch out for your eyes,' he said. 'This stuff can burn them out.'

It was the sort of story we told each other in the hope of making a dull job more interesting. There were tales of boys on the Shop who had amputated fingers while chopping firewood, an almost-authenticated account of a boot-repairer whose paring knife had slipped and castrated him, and an item of farm lore in which a boy sliding down a haystack failed to see the pitchfork below him and died screaming with the tines embedded in his bowels. Each time I heard it my spine chilled and my anus withered in sympathy. I professed not to believe it, but I never slid down haystacks.

I filled two buckets with whitewash and carried them to the privies. The walls of one were already stripped and a sour dust hung in the air. 'I'll need to wash my hair again,' said Spiff. 'Third bloody time this week.'

Capped with lime, he looked as though he was wearing a wig. 'Ray says you've got to watch this stuff,' I told him. 'It can burn you. Happen you'll go bald as well.'

He dusted himself off instantly. 'It stings.'

'I warned you. Perhaps it's coming out already.' I reached forward and gave his hair a tug. 'You see,' I said, sprinkling him with the stray hairs that clung to my fingers. 'It's coming out in handfuls.'

He grabbed me round the waist and we wrestled in the narrow passage. I shoved him into the gutter of the urinal and he twisted my right arm behind my back, forcing it between my shoulder blades. 'Give up!'

'Give up yourself.' I stamped on his foot and he hopped backwards and upset one of the buckets. The whitewash streamed over the flagstones and down the steps.

'Stop messing about,' shouted Ray, but it was too late. We both skidded and fell. I banged my head against the wall and Spiff sat in the second bucket. For a count of three he remained there, wedged with the whitewash lapping his thighs. Then he heaved himself out and began stripping off his trousers.

We all watched him, fascinated by the spectacle. 'What are you doing?' asked Doss as Spiff hurled the trousers into the nearest privy.

'You heard what he said. This stuff can burn you.' He peeled down his underpants and examined himself anxiously.

'Not there,' said Ray. 'It's your eyes you've got to watch.'

'Are you sure?'

Ray hesitated, reluctant to waste the moment. 'I think so.'

'Are you having me on?'

'Certainly not. It's the eyes where it does the most damage. But you don't want to take any chances. Think of your marriage prospects. Go and give it a wash.'

Spiff continued to peer at himself, unable to get close enough to the source of his anxiety. 'It's smarting,' he said.

I slid the empty bucket between his legs. 'That's to catch it if it drops off.'

'Ha bloody ha,' said Spiff. He seized the second bucket of whitewash and swung it by the handle. 'How would you like the same?'

'You wouldn't dare,' said Skelly.

'Wouldn't I?'

'You wouldn't be so bloody daft,' said Ray. He tried to grab the bucket but Spiff backed away, the whitewash splashing his thighs.

'He's going to do it,' said Doss. He ducked into the nearest privy and Ray and Skelly jumped after him. But I was too late. I saw the whitewash leap from the bucket like a long white tongue and instinctively I closed my eyes. It hit me in the chest, hard enough to send me backwards down the steps and I tottered into the yard witnessing the trail I left behind. It was a combination of splashes and footprints blanching the asphalt for several yards.

'Who wouldn't dare?' said Spiff.

Beneath the baggy legs of his underpants I saw his knees turning lilac with cold. His hair stood on end in dusty spikes and there was a smudge of dirt on his nose.

'Charles Atlas,' I said.

He pointed derisively at me. 'Mr Universe.'

Sister Beryl opened the back door and surveyed us both. 'What a pretty sight,' she said. 'What a pair of monkeys.'

My laughter died and I stroked the whitewash on my chest. 'We had an accident.'

'I can see that,' said Sister Beryl. 'Just the sort of accident I'd expect.' She folded her arms and barred the open doorway. 'You can clean yourselves up when you've finished the job. I'd make haste if I were you. That whitewash might spoil your beauty.' She stepped back and closed the door and I heard the key turn in the lock. Her apparent calm was much more alarming than one of her rages. She was saving up her anger until she could put it to good use.

The whitewash squelched in my shoes and I gestured towards the privies. 'We'd better get on with it then.'

'I'm bloody freezing,' said Spiff.

'I'm just the same.'

'I'll catch my death.'

'Not a chance,' said Ray. 'Just keep moving.' He jerked his head towards the kitchen door 'What d'you reckon she's up to?'

'Having a little chat with Mr Rome by now,' said Doss. He dialled a number in the air and spoke into a make-believe telephone. 'I have some wicked boys here. Dirty, disobedient; up to their arses in whitewash. Come right over and cane it off.' He replaced the receiver with a quiet 'ping'. 'Want to bet?'

Wearily, Ray shook his head. 'He'll be here right enough. Or we'll be over there. Which is worse?'

'Us over there,' said Skelly. 'I can't stand waiting outside that office. I can't stand waiting anyhow. Let's get the job done.'

It took us nearly three hours. Teatime came and went and

we were not called in. Small boys watched us through the dining room windows and we saw Sister Beryl drive them away. We were in isolation. The whitewash on my clothes caked like starch and my stiffened cuffs chafed my wrists. Finally Ray put down his brush. 'That's that,' he said.

The privies shone like hospital wards. Each cubicle glowed, white and holy. We had scrubbed the lavatory pans and washed down the flagstone. All the bad smells had been banished. Now it was a place of repose and meditation. We looked at our work with pride. 'You could eat your dinner off the floor,' said Skelly.

'Who'd want to do that?' said Doss.

'Joke over,' said Ray. 'I'll go and tell the old cow we've done.'

Sister Beryl was impressed; there was no doubt about that. She admired the walls and the ceilings and the shining earthenware. 'Very good,' she said. 'You see what you can do when you put your minds to it. It's a pity they'll most likely be pulling it all down.'

Spiff cocked his head to one side as if he had misheard. 'How's that?'

'It's not definite,' said Sister Beryl. 'But it's something we were discussing at a governor's meeting. Mr Buller thought they should be demolished. But now it's up to Mr Rome. I just thought we should make them look decent before he made up his mind. They're not slums, after all. We don't want to waste public money. People who make donations expect us to take care.'

I had never seen her look so pleasant or sound so reasonable. She pinched her nose with a handkerchief she plucked from her sleeve and the gentility of the gesture was as measured as her amiability.

'You mean we've spent all afternoon doing up those bogs just for Mr Rome to look them over?' demanded Ray.

'I wouldn't put it like that.'

'How would you put it?'

Sister Beryl sweetened her smile still further. 'I'd say you were doing as you were asked. Being helpful. Some of you at any rate.' She turned to me. 'You can wash those clothes out yourself. And his too. I know exactly who it was started that messing about. I've got eyes. Like I told you before, we know what's going on.'

'I'll wash my own things,' said Spiff.

'No you won't,' said Sister Beryl. 'And if you take my advice you'll not say another word. Nothing. Just keep your mouth shut and give your brain a chance to work.'

Her smile had vanished and her affability with it. She stood in her usual position – belly forward, hands on hips – and as if responding to some inner turbulence, strands of hair sprang loose from the mock tortoise-shell grips securing it on either side.

'Don't argue with her,' I said. 'You'll get no sense from a fool.'

She grabbed my shirt front. 'What did you say?'

'Deaf as well,' I said. I had drawn the lightning and felt it tingling in every nerve.

She slapped at my face and I caught her wrist. Ray put his hand on my shoulder but I shook it off. 'She started it.'

'I'll finish it too,' said Sister Beryl. 'Just you wait, my lad. You've gone too far this time. We'll see what Mr Rome has to say about this.'

'He can say what he likes.'

'I'll tell him that.'

'I bet you will. Telling tales is what you're good at.'

She wrenched her wrist free and I thought for a moment that she would try to hit me again. Instead, she smoothed her dress and composed herself. The gold rims of her spectacles glittered and there were beads of spittle on her lower lip. I could smell her cologne, as sweet as Dolly Mixtures. 'Right you are,' she said. 'We'll see about this.'

She marched across the yard and we followed her in through the back door. We heard the distant ring and rattle of the telephone and then we saw her, dressed in her coat and hat, crossing the road towards the governor's house.

'Bloody hell,' said Spiff. 'You've done it this time.'

I was not sure what I had done. My aversion to Sister

Beryl was so strong that I could not imagine reacting in any other way. It was cause and effect, as simple as pressing a switch and making light. My horseplay with Spiff had given her the excuse to complain, even to punish. But it seemed to release a deeper resentment, a hoarded dislike which swept away the caution I had nurtured so carefully. Her malice was an insult which had to be returned. The impulse was stronger than logic. I could no longer remain silent. It made my head swim like inhaling gas at the dentist's. I still felt giddy and unrepentant.

The feeling persisted, even when I was called into the sitting room where Mr Rome stood with his back to the fire. His expression was mournful and he sighed when he saw me. 'What did you say when we last met?' he enquired. 'Something about your spot of bother being all over?'

'That's right, sir.'

'But what's this that Sister Beryl's been telling me? Rudeness? Refusing to do as you're told? Damaging clothes? What have you got to say about all that?'

I stared at the floor. 'She made me.'

'I don't follow.'

'She did it on purpose. She got us whitewashing the privies when they're to be pulled down. She wasted our free time. She started shouting. She thinks she's the only one who's allowed to be rude.'

I realised that my voice was raised and I swallowed hard. 'I meant what I said. I thought it was all over. I don't want to be in trouble.' To my dismay I felt tears flood my eyes.

Mr Rome waited for several seconds but I could not go on. 'Is that all?'

'That's all, sir.'

'And you don't care what I have to say. Is that right?'

'I didn't mean that. She's twisting words again.' My exhilaration was spent. I retreated into silence and with my eyes lowered, watched the glossy toe-caps of Mr Rome's shoes see-saw on the carpet as he rocked himself backwards and forwards in front of the fire. The shoes were beautifully waxed and abstractedly I found myself wondering what brand of polish he used. It was a subject in which my mother was deeply interested and at home the rival merits of Wren and Kiwi and Cherry Blossom were always being discussed.

My speculations came to an abrupt end as Mr Rome jogged to rest. 'I gather that you and Sister Beryl don't get on.'

'No sir.'

'Have you never got on?'

'No sir.'

'Would you say you were a reasonable person?'

The question was unexpected, but twisting it this way and that I could detect no booby-trap. 'Yes sir,' I said.

'I imagine Sister Beryl would describe herself in the same way.'

I did not reply and he sighed more deeply than before. 'I'm afraid you are what is known as incompatible,' he said. 'Of course you were rude and of course you were disobedient. But you already know that. Punishment won't help. The important thing is to ensure it doesn't happen again.'

He crossed over to the window and surveyed the road as if seeking inspiration in the broad sweep of tarmac, blotted with oil where the buses waited, shining now beneath summer rain. 'I must give it some thought,' he said. 'It is not an occasion for rushing to judgement.'

Forty-eight hours later his mind was made up. When I came home from school Sister Beryl met me at the front door. 'You're to pack your case and report to Mr Rome's office. Don't dawdle and don't leave anything behind.'

'Where am I going?'

'That's for Mr Rome to tell you,' she said.

I could not decide whether she was pleased or not. Nothing less than a court martial and a public flogging would have given her total satisfaction, I thought. But she was unmistakably relieved at the prospect of being rid of me.

I said goodbye to Sister Joyce who punched me in the chest, jovially but harder than was necessary, and reported to Mr Rome. His face was as long as ever. It was as though somewhere within his chest there was a repository of bad news, so distressing that only one item at a time was released to plague him daily. The supply, though, was endless and he grieved both in retrospect and in anticipation. I felt guilty for adding to his worries.

'I'm moving you on,' he said without delay. 'It seems the only thing to do. Don't think of it as a victory or defeat, simply as a solution. I am placing you in Franklin House with Sister Emma and Sister Kathleen. They are younger women than Sister Beryl and perhaps not so conservative in their attitudes. Do not, however, think for one moment that you can take advantage of them. They have my complete support. It is you who will be on trial and it is you who will suffer if you let me down.'

We shook hands and he sighed. 'Look to your sense of responsibility,' he said. 'Think of your future.'

Together we walked to his car and he drove me the few hundred yards to my new home. I knew the reason now for Sister Beryl's mixed feelings. I had not been punished. I had been given another chance, even granted a new status. My move was the first indication of a new policy. I was Mr Rome's experiment.

Nine

SISTER EMMA helped me to make my bed. 'I'd give you a room to yourself but we're a bit crowded at present,' she said. 'There's only this little boy who sleeps in the corner. He's just a baby really. He won't bother you. You won't be disturbed.'

'Of course not.'

'And I'll want you to keep the others quiet. Like a prefect. There were prefects at your other school I expect.'

'Yes, there were. Not me. I was too young.'

'Well you're not too young now. Remember what Mr Rome said about taking responsibility.'

'I'll remember,' I said.

Sister Emma was new to the branch. She was tall and buxom with dark hair curled trimly round her head like a pie crust. She had a crooning, West-country voice and an air of unquenchable good humour. Her deputy, Sister Kathleen, was also dark but her hair was long and wired with grey and she had anxious brown eyes in a pale face. She reminded me of a Brontë heroine from the books we had recently started to read at school.

'You can use our bathroom if you like,' said Sister Emma. 'Have you started shaving yet?'

I stroked my chin. 'Two or three times a week.'

'You can keep your razor on the shelf by the toothbrushes. And don't leave your bristles in the basin.'

'I won't,' I said. 'I always clean up after me.'

'Then we'll get on fine,' said Sister Emma.

The boy with whom I was sharing the bedroom was named Roddy James. He was six years old and uncommonly drowsy. Even during the day he sat with his chin on his chest, either dozing or about to nod off. At night he was always fast asleep when I came to bed, his thumb jammed in his mouth, small snores oozing from his nose. I scarcely noticed him; it was like having a room of my own. There were curtains at the window, a coat hanger behind the door and even a bookcase on which I arranged my *Observer Book of British Birds* and *The Collected Poems of John Masefield*. Beneath my mattress were two sheets of stout cardboard.

'If you put your trousers between them when you go to bed you'll keep your creases,' said Sister Emma. 'You want to look smart, don't you?'

I was overwhelmed. No one had ever shown me such consideration, nor was it extended only to me. We were all encouraged to invite boys from other houses to tea and there was no lack of takers. At Franklin House the food was distinctly better than standard branch fare. Every evening Sister Emma filled a large shallow basin with milk which she put in the bottom oven. By the morning it was covered by a thick crust of clotted cream which we ate with strawberry jam. She made savoury dishes with cheese, and cakes which were shared scrupulously to the last crumb.

Sister Emma enjoyed her food. She ate with a dainty greed, forcing herself to chew each mouthful the statutory number of times before loading her fork again. Sometimes I heard her sigh when she finished a meal as if the pleasure was too intense to curtail. She was inclined to put on weight and limited herself to one slice of toast in the morning, two potatoes for lunch and half a spoonful of sugar in her tea. But if someone else served her with more than her self-imposed ration she would not give it back. It was an accident from which she felt morally entitled to benefit.

Mr Rome had emphasised the importance of my having a quiet place in which to do my homework and she offered me her sitting room.

'But you'll want it yourself,' I said. 'And Sister Kathleen's got her piano there.'

'We can manage,' said Sister Emma.

'I won't need it that much.'

'You will if you do the work you're supposed to.'

'I can read in bed.'

'Yes,' she said doubtfully, 'you can do that, I suppose. But I don't want you straining your eyes.'

Her concern was almost too much to assimilate. It was feast after famine and it unsettled me. I was also prey to waves of suspicion which woke me sometimes in the middle of the night as if the boat in which I had been dreaming was being swept in a direction I had not charted by some unseen but powerful impulse. I did not know where Sister Emma was taking me. 'Do you have a girl friend?' she asked me one day.

'Sort of.'

'What does that mean?'

'She's leaving soon. She's off to London.'

'Will you miss her?'

'I expect so.'

'What about girls at school?'

'They're different, I couldn't have a real girl friend at school. It wouldn't work.'

'Why on earth not?'

I thought of the extraordinary caste system we all observed and decided against trying to explain it. 'It's too complicated.'

'They're no better than you are,' said Sister Emma.

'I know that.'

'Wasn't your mother a teacher?'

'A head-mistress.'

'There you are then.' She was darning socks, patiently weaving a thatch of grey wool over a wooden mushroom. 'Dratted thing,' she said. 'It's going to be more darn than sock by the time I'm finished.'

'My mother gets headaches when she does that.'

'She's not missing much.' She completed the darn and fitted the mushroom beneath the next hole. 'Isn't it time you went to see her?'

'I wouldn't mind.'

'Is that all?'

I dug my hands into my pockets and kicked at the hearth rug. 'I just wish she wouldn't write those letters.'

'What letters?'

'Telling people how much she wants to see me. Getting them in a state about helping her.'

Sister Emma put down the darning mushroom. 'I've never heard of any letters.'

'Honestly?'

'Honestly. I just thought it was time you went home on a visit. It's been over a year.'

'Eighteen months,' I said. 'She's been writing to my friend's mother. And *she* says she's going to write to Mr Rome. She even said she'd pay my fare, but I asked her not to.'

'I should hope not,' said Sister Emma. She re-threaded her needle and plunged it into the darn. 'We'd better get a move on then. You break up next month. I'll try and have a word with Mr Rome tomorrow.'

It was all arranged by the following week. The day after we broke up for the summer holidays I was to go home for a fortnight. 'Pass it on to your mother,' I told Phil Watson. 'There's no need for her to write now.'

'She'll be glad,' he said.

'Everybody's glad.' I longed for people to show a little less interest. The scrutiny was too intense.

'It's not going to be as bad as all that,' said Sister Emma when I sulkily accepted a clean shirt to wear for the journey.

'You don't know my mother.'

'Well don't go with a face like that. You'd turn milk sour. Give her a smile.' She pinched my cheek. 'Look on the bright side.'

My mother had aged dramatically since I last saw her. The blue of her eyes had faded and one side of her hair was a blaze of silver, marking the dent in her skull where the surgeon had removed the brain tumour. She refused to use the walking stick which the doctor had prescribed and hobbled about the house, clinging to the sideboard, the table and the backs of chairs like a mountaineer clambering over a rock face.

'She won't be told,' complained Mary. 'She had a nasty fall last week.'

'Don't fuss,' said my mother.

'Someone needs to fuss.'

'No they don't. I can manage.'

Mary snorted like the coalman's horse I once gave my apple cores to. 'I'm the one who has to manage. Who was it had to haul you up them stairs when you came a cropper on Monday?'

'I could have got up myself.'

'You can tell that to the marines.'

'I didn't ask you to help.'

'You'd have just lain there then.' She folded her arms and the safety pins securing her modesty vest bobbed into view. 'Honestly, there's times I don't know what to do. You break a leg and it's me that'll have to tell Mr Barlow.'

Mr Barlow was my Uncle Ernest, a droll, sardonic man whose opinions my mother held in awe. He was her eldest brother and the authority born of her childhood still endured. 'There's no need to worry him,' she said. 'He's got enough on his plate as it is.'

'Then don't you go adding to it.'

My mother shooed her away. 'Just get on with what you're doing. Stop mithering about me.'

They were like an old married couple, I thought, nagging each other with love and exasperation, complaining to whoever else would listen, eking out their small budget, fearful that money or health would fail unless it was constantly tended. They had planned my favourite meals. There were lamb chops for lunch and a steak and kidney pie already in the oven. There was a banana custard cooling on the bottom step of the larder ('I queued for twenty minutes to get them bananas,' Mary told me) and from a food parcel sent by my uncle in America my mother had saved a tin of spam.

She weighed it in her hands and passed it to me to admire. 'You'll not have anything like this at school,' she said.

'Not at the Homes. We do sometimes at school. For lunches with salad.'

'What's the difference?' she said sharply. 'When you're away from here you're at school.'

I shook my head. 'The Homes are where I live and the school's in Darwen. It's a train ride away. It's not the same at all.'

'You know what I mean,' said my mother. 'You're just being difficult. It confuses people telling them you're in two places at once. If you tell them you're away at school that's good enough. It complicates things otherwise.'

I looked at her for a long time before replying. Was she really so disingenuous or had she convinced herself that the Homes and the school were somehow joined? 'I don't mind what you tell people,' I said at last. 'But if they don't understand I'll have to explain.'

'Of course you will. Anyway, you'll not be there much longer.'

'Two years or so.'

'That's not long. It'll soon pass. And then you'll be home for good.'

I said nothing and my mother gave me an affectionate shake. 'Won't that be nice.'

'I'm not sure what I'll be doing.'

'Not sure? Of course you're sure. Your place is here. It's what your father wanted. "Don't worry, Connie," he used to say, "you've got the boy to look after you." They were almost his last words.'

'He didn't know what it was going to be like,' I said. 'I might not be able to get the work I want around here.'

'What's that?'

'Newspapers,' I said. 'English is my best subject. They think I should go in for journalism.'

My mother tossed the *Evening Sentinel* into my lap. 'We've got papers here.'

'I know,' I said. 'But I was thinking of London. That's where my friends will be.'

'What friends?' My mother's face was already flushed. Any suggestion, real or imagined, that the district in which she was born and bred failed to meet all demands made her hackles rise.

'People I've met at the Homes. They're going to London to work. I want to keep in touch.'

'You've heard of writing letters, I suppose.'

'That's not what I mean. I want to see them.'

'They're more important to you than I am?'

'That's not the point.' It was too soon to have this discussion. I had not meant to allow the subject to arise. The idea of becoming a journalist was still fairly new to me. It had first come up during a discussion about careers in one of Mr Gaskell's infinitely variable Religious Instruction lessons and I had seized upon it without exactly knowing why. Newspaper reporters in films were high on my list of heroes. I had just seen *Thunder Rock* in which foreign correspondent Michael Redgrave had tried vainly to warn the world of the rise of Nazi Germany, and I responded to his blend of idealism and despair. I was also at ease with words, enjoying them for their own sake. To earn a living by developing a skill I already possessed struck me as highly desirable. It also seemed to offer an independence I could not yet visualise. But I was certain about one thing. The miracle would take place in London. I was determined not to return home.

'What is the point then?' demanded my mother. 'Who are these friends that are so important?'

'You don't know them.'

'I don't suppose I ever will. Not if you're in London and I'm stuck here.'

It was happening, just as I had feared. My mother still dreamed dreams in which all promises were kept and all endings were happy. She was able to exclude betrayals to which she had been party. She had done what was right and by demurring, however tentatively, I was denying her justice, the proper reward for good behaviour. I felt sick with guilt, but I could not back down. I tried to deflect her rage. 'I'm not there yet. Anything could happen.'

'I know that. I might die. That'd be handy.'

She flopped down on the couch by the window and stared into our small garden. The hedges needed cutting. Fronds of privet trailed down on to the baked earth and lupin pods, their flowers shrivelled away, caught the sun like grey velvet wallets.

'Don't be daft,' I said. 'You're not going to die.'

'A fat lot you care.'

'Of course I care.'

'Prove it then.'

'There's no point in talking about it.' I thought longingly of Sadie, jammed between the office cupboards, her body churning against mine. It was like a charm, a spell which I could invoke for my protection. She was an alternative, an antidote I could safely tap so long as it remained hidden. 'I'll tidy up the garden,' I said.

'You needn't bother. You won't be here to see it.'

It was too much. 'You made sure of that,' I said.

My mother's head swung round as if I had tugged on a lead. 'It's no use blaming me. It's your own fault you were expelled from your proper school. Saying those wicked things. What else did you expect? You could have gone to prison. Your Uncle Percy said so. Criminal libel, he said. You needn't feel sorry for yourself. If anyone's to blame for how things are, it's you.'

I stormed out into the garden and attacked the hedges, shearing the sooty leaves and releasing clouds of midges which followed me in a cloud, hanging over my head as I barbered the privet, drowning themselves in the sweat which poured down my face.

Mary called me in for lunch. 'Your mother's had to lie down,' she said. 'You should be ashamed of yourself, upsetting her like that.'

'She started it.'

'It doesn't matter who started it. You know what she's

like. Let's hope she doesn't have an attack.'

'Does she have them often?'

'More than she used to. I had to fetch the doctor last week, she was so bad.'

'And what did he say?'

Mary sliced into her lamb chop and doused it with mint sauce. 'He said she wasn't to get excited. I thought she'd explode. "What's there for me to get excited about?" she said. "Sitting here like a cabbage." He gave her some stronger tablets.'

'That's all?'

'What else could he do? You're not here. You don't know what she's like. She can be a right terror.'

'I know that.'

'You don't know the half of it. Just think yourself lucky you're off and away.'

'It's where she sent me. I didn't ask to go.'

'That can't be helped.' She chewed on a scrap of gristle, stripping off the meat before placing it neatly on the side of her plate. 'Make the best of it, that's my advice to you. Don't argue with her. Don't let her get you rattled.'

It was the longest speech I had ever heard her make and I was impressed. She had learned the knack of living with my mother and the rules she spelled out made sense. For the rest of the holiday I tried to avoid scenes. I called on all my uncles and aunts, adhering to a time-table worked out by my mother. I haunted the cinemas for miles around, sometimes seeing three films in one day and pretending when I got home that I had spent the time walking to Brown Edge or Congleton, country rambles of which my mother approved. On Sundays I attended morning service at Hill Top chapel, sharing a pew with my Uncle Arthur who made shorthand notes on the sermon in his diary before falling into a deep sleep from which he was roused by a blast from the organ announcing the closing hymn.

It became clear that most of my relations were embarassed by any reference to the Homes. A Bluecoat school was one thing, but a proper orphanage open to destitutes and incorrigibles was another. The compromise, anticipated by my mother, was to talk about the grammar school and friends such as Phil Watson whose status was much the same as our own. I found myself endorsing a curious fiction in which I was a boarder at a day school, performing mysterious tasks on my days off for which I was not paid but which, in sometimes quite specific ways, contributed to the war effort. I was working on the land. I was helping to Dig for Victory. I was a member of the Air Training Corps. My patriotism served to disguise the social anomalies.

My Uncle Ernest, however, was not deceived. 'What's it like then, butcher?' he asked, using one of his pet names for me which he had adopted for no other reason than to annoy my Uncle Percy.

'I've got used to it now,' I said.

'Bad as that, is it?'

'Sometimes. I don't mind school, but I can't stick the Homes.'

He raised an eyebrow. 'Looks like tha'll have to stick it.'

'I expect so.'

'And then what?'

My mother, I reasoned, had already told him her plans for my future. 'There's talk of me coming home.'

'But what do you say?'

I shook my head. 'I don't think so.'

'I thought as much.' He filled his pipe, shredding the flake in the palm of his hand and feeding it, pinch by pinch, into the tarry bowl.

'Mary says I shouldn't argue. It only upsets my mother.'

He struck a match and lowered it on to the tobacco. The room filled with sweet wreaths of smoke and he peered at me through the fug. 'Your mother always frets when she doesn't get her own way. She did as a girl.'

'She says my dad told her I'd look after her.'

'Very likely. But you're not bound by that. I knew your father, remember. He wouldn't want to burden you. He'd just want you to do your best.'

I said nothing, stifled by a surge of love. My Uncle Ernest continued: 'We'd have had you here if we could. You must know that. But it's not possible. Your auntie's not well and I'm an old crock. But we'd never turn you away. Not if you couldn't manage.'

His back was to the window and his face was lost in shadow and pipe smoke. 'I'll manage,' I said.

'I reckon you will.' He leaned forward and clasped my knee. 'And make up your own mind what you do. There's no one can tell you. It's your life. You've got to live it.' He slackened his grip and I saw his nails, one bruised by a badly aimed hammer, another sawn across the cuticle. It was the hand of a man who earned his bread by toiling for others. I believed what he said. He did not require me to invent stories about school.

I tried to will the time to go quickly. If I went out my mother demanded to know where I was going and when I came back, questioned me fiercely about whom I had seen. It was not mere curiosity. It was vital for her to feel that she remained in contact with the world outside and I became her eyes, her agent who not only reported on events but represented her interests. On fine days she would make her way slowly round the garden, leaning heavily on the detested stick, but she would never go beyond the front gate. Her left leg was grotesquely swollen, the laces of her shoe barely met and she dragged it behind her like a baulk of timber. Looking through a copy of the *National Geographic* magazine sent to us from America she saw a photograph of elephants hauling teak. One of them, a rogue male, was chained to a tree trunk to prevent him running amok. 'That's me,' she said, jabbing the picture with her finger, 'stuck here for ever.'

She urged me to seek out my old friends, but we had grown apart. We no longer shared the same jokes or the same experiences. When they discussed future plans, whether it was going to a football match or an expedition to

Trentham Gardens, we all realised that I would not be there to join them. They did not wish to exclude me, but we lived in different worlds.

The day before I was due to return to the Homes my mother showed me three small parcels, wrapped in tissue paper. The first contained a set of lace dressing-table mats for Mrs Watson. There was a box of writing paper for Sister Emma and in the third there was a packet of handkerchiefs. 'That's for Mr Rome,' she said. 'To show my appreciation.'

I was horrified. 'No one gives the governor presents.'

'I don't see why not. He's taken a real interest in you.'

'It's his job,' I said.

'All the more reason to say thank you.'

I could not explain how unsuitable the gesture was. Not that my mother would have listened. She was demonstrating yet again that like could speak to like, that understanding could be reached. If the gift was acknowledged she had opened a line of communication. She was no longer simply another parent but a caring and invalid mother who deserved special consideration.

Her presents reminded me that I had not bought anything for Sadie. Jewellery of some sort was called for: a locket or a bracelet perhaps. But I was short of money and there was no one who could supply it. I caught the bus to Hanley and, without much hope, inspected the windows of Pidduck & Beardmore, the town's biggest jewellers. The prices made my heart sink. There was nothing there I could afford. I walked on to Webberley's, the bookshop which also had a gift department. It was the same story. There were tortoise-shell boxes and onyx paperweights and pen-holders made of marble. Everything was expensive; nothing was suitable.

I wandered upstairs into the section selling Bibles and hymnals and between a display of books by Patience Strong offering short passages of inspirational verse printed as prose and the collected works of H.V. Morton, whose travels in the Holy Land was the only best-seller my Uncle Arthur had ever bought, I saw what I wanted. On a strip of black cloth lay a row of crucifixes. Most of them were of plain metal, but the one which caught my eye was made of ebony on which a silver Christ hung in torment. It was attached to a silver chain and it looked both chaste and expensive.

There was one attendant at the far end of the room. Her back was turned as she dusted a showcase and almost without thinking I slipped the crucifix into my pocket. My heart hammered at the base of my throat and I skimmed through several pages of Patience Strong while I regained my composure. I was not in any sense religious, despite my father having been a lay preacher. At the Bluecoat school I had sung in the choir, but my beliefs were perfunctory. I attended morning assembly and church services but I did not worship. God, if He existed, was someone like an associate of Mr Rome or whoever decided whether I should be called up for military service. Prayers were as futile as letters posted to Father Christmas. The concept of Life Eternal seemed absurd unless there was some guarantee that it would be easier or more exciting than life temporal.

On the other hand I saw no reason to disbelieve in ghosts, and magic, as everyone knew, was real. If it was not, I wanted it to be. There were no other means that I could conjecture of fulfilling my most ardent desires. In the local museum, less than half a mile away, there were masks and fetishes which were reputed to have been used in voodoo rituals. With our noses pressed to the glass case we had tried to will them into action, as if by staring long and hard enough we could switch on their power like a wireless set. Occasionally, when some unexpected bounty was awaiting me at home, I wondered if we had succeeded. It gave me a creepy feeling.

So did the crucifix. As good Methodists my family abhorred the trappings of papistry. They were pagan, said my mother, like beads worn by savages. They did not accord with her notion of God as a healthy, fair-minded liberal who drank water from the tap and preferred boiled beef to pheasant. Our God would have no truck with incense or trinkets. He was a plain man who preferred to be worshipped plainly. But, clutching the crucifix in my jacket pocket, I felt common sense desert me. Although I practised no religion I knew I had blasphemed. Not only was I a thief, but what I had stolen was an object at least as potent as the fetishes we had viewed with such awe in the museum. My own lack of faith was irrelevant. It was enough that others believed. Even the prayers at Hill Top directed the wrath of God on to evil-doers. I sensed it hanging over me like a thunder cloud ready to break and point to my guilt with a shaft of lightning.

I was already at the shop door. No one had stopped or spoken to me. I stepped into the street and sighed with relief. But the anxiety did not go away. I walked round Hanley market and spent half an hour in the loft where canaries sang in cages bright with chromium and dogs, most of them mongrels, stared through thickets of chicken wire, their muzzles resting on their paws. There were tassels and sacks of birdseed for sale and goldfish swimming through coral arcades and rabbits, their ears flattened and their noses twitching as if they were about to sneeze. It had always been a favourite place of mine. I liked to grip the cast-iron balustrade like a ship's captain standing on his bridge and survey the market below. Each stall wore a coronet of coloured lights. There were smells of earth and sacking and boiled sweets and apples which blended into a pungent and comfortable aroma which I usually found soothing. Not today; the sharp points of the crucifix dug into my hand and my fingertips traced the shape of the hanging body. Even as I watched the shoppers I could recall the tilt of the crown of thorns and the anguish distorting the silver face. I knew I had to take it back.

There were more customers in Webberleys than there had been earlier on. In the religious books section a man and a woman were examining book-markers. They had covered one counter with their selection, all of them vellum, printed with flowers and a suitable text from the Bible or one of the Great Poets.

'Wordsworth, do you think?' said the man.

'Is there nothing more modern?' said the woman. 'I can't bear those daffodils.'

They rummaged more deeply in the box and the assistant smiled through her teeth. She saw me hovering near Patience Strong and took a step forward. 'Can I be of assistance?'

'No thank you.'

'You're sure you are in the right department?'

'Quite sure.'

She did not seem at all convinced and continued to dart glances in my direction between arbitrating on the book-markers. I had to take a chance. I palmed the crucifix and as I slid it from my pocket, turned to face the assistant. She was not looking and without moving from where I stood I reached out and put the crucifix back from where I had taken it. At that moment the assistant raised her head but my hand was empty.

'Exactly what is it you're looking for?' she enquired.

'A present of some sort,' I said vaguely. 'I'll think about it.

A weight had gone from my chest. I could breathe again. I walked jauntily out of the shop and swaggered to the bus stop. Humility would have been more fitting, I realised, but my reprieve filled me with elation. I did not have the forethought to disguise it in some way before meeting my mother.

'Glad you're going back, I see,' she said.

'No I'm not. It's just that it's a nice day.'

'I hadn't noticed,' said my mother. 'You don't see much from inside four walls.'

'Would you like me to take a chair outside?'

'I can't stand the sun on my head. You know that.' Unconsciously she stroked the silver blaze in her hair and I remembered that she had almost died in hospital. Pioneer surgery, my Aunt Ada had called it. But it had left her a crippled and desolate woman. 'I miss you,' she said. 'All the time. I feel cheated. I'm not watching you grow up.

Each time I see you, you're different. I hardly know you now.'

'I'm just the same.'

'No you're not. You can't pretend. You never tell me what you're really thinking. You shut me out.'

My eyes stung. It was not fair, I thought. I did not want to hurt her but there was nothing I could say that would give her comfort. 'I love you,' I said.

'In your own way.'

I put my arms round her and breathed in the lavender scent of her cardigan. Muslin bags of it were tucked in among her clothes. She suffered my embrace but did not return it. 'Have you done your packing?' she asked.

'There's not much to do.'

'You don't want to leave it till the last minute.'

'I won't.'

'Don't forget the presents. I'll put them in your case.'

I hugged her again, then let her go. As if she could read my mind she said, 'These friends of yours in London; are they boys or girls?'

'Both. There's no one special. Just people I know.'

She repeated the phrase, making it sound even more hollow than before. 'There are people you know here. What is it that makes London the be-all and end-all?'

'It's where the work is.'

'That's not what you said before.'

'It's true though.'

Our eyes met and held. It was not the end of the argument, but a point had been made and taken. My mother knew it was not the whole truth, but I would not back down from it.

'There's years yet,' she said. 'Anything can happen.'

'Anything at all.'

'You might even go to university.'

It was a debate I did not wish to enter. 'I doubt it.'

'They might not want you,' she said and we both smiled.

The next day I caught the train from Stoke and travelled north. In Manchester I bought Sadie a gold locket shaped like a heart with money my Uncle Arthur had given me when I called to say goodbye and at Bolton I boarded the bus to the Homes. We drove past pit wheels and mill chimneys, through the village and on to the ridge where my Uncle Percy's hat had blown off, and as we turned the corner I saw Argyle House to my right and further back the white flag of steam flying from the laundry chimney. It was very odd, I thought. I was not unhappy. I was not even homesick. I was on familiar ground. I was back where I belonged.

Ten

ON THE LAST DAY of September everyone turned out for potato-lifting. It was not a job like hay-making in which everything depended on fine weather, but there were three big meadows to clear and Mr King's ambition was to complete the task within a week before the autumn rains bogged the tractor down in mud which made driving impossible.

Rain was falling as we trooped into the first field. A thick white mist sprawled down from the moors and a flock of gulls following the tractor dived in and out of it as if they were part of some conjuring trick, multiplying or dividing their numbers each time they reappeared. There was a stink of exhaust fumes and Ray grabbed my arm. 'Watch out,' he said.

Whirling steel prongs dug under the potato haulms showering us with earth and vegetables and, as he roared past us, Mr King pretended not to notice. He was wearing his tractor jacket, a reversible raincoat solid with grease which had been given to him by Mr Buller. Beneath it he wore a waistcoat, a pullover and a woolly cardigan. His hat was pulled down over his ears and his pipe was jammed in his mouth. He had the fixed expression of a man on a mission, sworn to carry out his duty whatever the cost. Perched behind him, Doss waved with one hand while he clung to the driver's seat with the other. The tractor lurched over a half-buried rock and he almost fell off.

'There was a lad killed just like that,' said Ray cheerfully. 'The spikes went clean through him. He was dead before they got him to hospital.'

We each took a sack from a pile beside the petrol cans and started the long plod to the far end of the meadow. The

potatoes lay all around us, greasy with mud and after five
minutes of picking them up my fingers were numb.
Someone had lit a fire of potato haulms but it was too soon
to stop and warm ourselves.

'Only pick the big ones,' said Ray.

'What about the others?'

'Tread 'em in.' He filled his sack before me and tied the
neck with baling twine. The rain had slackened but mist
now swathed the meadow from end to end. Beads of
condensation clung to my jacket like seed pearls and Ray's
quiff sagged wetly on to his forehead. The tractor
chuntered invisibly to my left and to my right I could see
lines of stooped figures marking where it had been.

After an hour I thought my back would break but when I
stretched myself I heard Mr King bawling at me in the
distance. 'Get on with it there. Grammar-school boys
included!'

It was not ill meant. Mr King's commands were as
automatic as drill instructions. We paused; he shouted.
Grammar-school boys meant boys who thought
themselves superior. It was a convention which he
accepted without questioning whether or not it was true,
but also without feeling impelled to abuse us for our
supposed snobbery. It may have been pure laziness which
saved him from being vindictive. He found malice was
exhausting and disliked having to expend himself
unnecessarily. He did not like Sister Beryl because she tried
to co-opt him in punitive measures, such as finding boys
extra work to do which would also have meant extra
supervision. But he was deeply suspicious of the new order
represented by Mr Rome and by the Sisters of Franklin
House.

'Clotted cream for tea!' he exclaimed when I was rash
enough to brag about our improved menu. 'They'll be
knitting you bed socks next!'

'Bright red with bobbles on,' said Ray, who somehow felt
that my removal from Mosscrop rated as preferential
treatment. All the same, he came for tea when he was

invited and when I produced a bag of scones at our mid-morning break he perked up and looked hopeful.

Instead, I offered the bag to Mr King. 'Sister Emma made them.'

'Go on!' He was genuinely surprised. The Sisters that he knew did not send their boys to work with bags of home-made scones. He took one and nibbled it suspiciously. 'Very good,' he said.

I gave one to Ray who wolfed it down. 'What's old Pod doing?' I asked.

'Same as usual. She had a row with Joyce last week. Wanted to stop the dancing classes. Silly old bag.'

Through the mist two boys appeared carrying an urn of cocoa between them. We hurried over to be first in the queue. It was not our favourite drink, but the damp had soaked through to our bones. We had covered less than a third of the meadow and we would be there until late afternoon. 'Sister Emma reckons we shouldn't have to do jobs like this,' I said.

Ray licked off his cocoa moustache. 'Why not?'

'She says we do our week's work like everyone else, so we're entitled to time off.'

'They'll never stand for that,' said Ray.

'She'll try.'

I had never heard Sister Emma raise her voice, but she was both eloquent and determined. She was a big woman and when she entered an argument it was with a massive composure which seemed almost to soothe her opponents into capitulating. She was aware of her size and always sat neatly, with her feet together and her hands in her lap as if by being tidy she could tuck away the extra inches. She was not fat. Her arms and legs, though substantial, were firm and well shaped. She did not wobble when she walked, but swayed rhythmically from side to side as though she was shifting ballast beneath her tightly buttoned coat. When she told stories her voice would sometimes fade at the end of the sentence, signalling a gulp of laughter which she tried to stopper with a hand to her mouth. Her good humour was infectious. I did not think of her as a teacher or an agent of authority but as a woman. As Mr Rome had implied she was younger than most of the other Sisters and she was dedicated, not to an institution but to a way of life which she had chosen for herself.

She tried to be impartial but she was not afraid to declare her loyalties. She wrote to thank my mother for the box of writing paper but she would not join her campaign to persuade me to return home when I left school. 'It's up to you,' she said. 'I've told her so. It's too soon to talk about duty. You've got to get through those examinations. That's quite enough to be going on with.'

'Did you tell her that too?'

'I said you had a lot of work to do. I said you had to concentrate.'

She was perfectly sincere but, unintentionally, it was she who created distractions. Sharing the Sisters' bathroom – Emma's intimation that I should consider myself as an adult and consequently behave like one – was a luxury which I enjoyed. But it bred an intimacy which took me by surprise. Stockings hung out to dry over the bath reminded me of the flesh they covered. There were jars of hand cream and flasks of talc by the wash-basin. Once I found a single hair, as curly as a watch spring, in the bath and an instant and unbidden erection parted my pyjamas. I did not dare leave the bathroom until it had gone down. Sister Kathleen rattled the doorknob and I splashed water in the basin.

'You'll miss the bus if you don't hurry.'

'In a minute.' I applied a cold flannel without success.

'They're sitting down to breakfast. Get a move on.'

I took off my pyjama jacket and draped it over my arm. The bulge was still there but barely discernible. 'I'm coming now.'

She stepped aside to let me cross the landing. 'You'll have to be quicker than this,' she said. 'It's not fair to everyone else.'

Often I had the feeling that Sister Kathleen regarded me as an intruder who had created an imbalance, possibly dangerous, within the house. She and Emma were friends as well as colleagues and a third person, still clumsily adolescent but indulged as an adult, was an oddity with whom it was hard to be at ease. My use of the bathroom and sitting room were incursions on her privacy. She tried not to resent me but I usurped time and space which were rightly hers and by threatening her leisure and privacy I threatened her work. She was less tolerant, less giving than she wished to be. I made her dislike herself and consequently she disliked me.

Sister Emma would have none of it. 'It's your imagination,' she said when I told her I would rather they kept their sitting room to themselves.

'No it's not. She doesn't want me there. I'm not blaming her but it makes me feel funny.'

'Everything makes you feel funny.'

She ruffled my hair and I drew back. 'I've just combed it.'

'Vanity,' she said. 'You're as bad as Raymond Clutton.'

'Nobody is. I've seen him spend half an hour getting his quiff right.'

'You don't need to do that,' said Sister Emma. 'It's perfectly nice as it is.'

She reached out to touch me again and I dodged behind the table. It was not my hair I was trying to protect; the teasing threatened to bring back my erection. It was a hazard against which I constantly had to be on guard. Riding on the tops of trams produced it. So did reading some of the paperbacks on sale in Darwen market. There was a book of sex instruction by Dr Rennie McAndrew called *The Red Light*. The title itself was provocative. So was the text, despite its high moral tone. Merely the naming of parts induced a *frisson* which, in the bleak terminology of Dr McAndrew, resulted in an engorgement of the spongy tissue of the penis and, although it helped me to understand the nature of my affliction, it did not tell me how to prevent it.

I had realised from the start that by sending me to a house which was run on so-called progressive lines Mr Rome was taking a calculated risk. His ideas were not popular with the old guard. Unlike Mr Buller who had rattled the tinfoil of revolution but left the packet unopened, Mr Rome was already distributing the contents. One of his first concessions was to allow the older boys and girls to leave the branch on Sunday afternoon walks without supervision. We were also excused the Sunday morning parade although we had to make our way to the chapel in an accompanying group and attend the service. He encouraged us to listen to the wireless and discuss the programmes we heard. He introduced monthly socials and funded the purchase of a radiogram and a small library of records. The innovations increased and the senior sisters led by Sister Agnes and Sister Beryl predicted disaster.

As one of Mr Rome's guinea-pigs I was under especially close scrutiny. Sometimes I felt like the wild boy of France to whom we were introduced in one of Mr Gaskell's more eccentric Religious Instruction lessons – happily living on nuts and berries, pining when a well-intentioned doctor tried to domesticate him. I did not pine at Franklin House but I was unsettled in ways which it was tactful to conceal. I told no one of what had happened in the bathroom. When Sadie asked me if it was true that Emma and Kathleen walked about the house wearing only their dressing gowns I made a joke of it and described garments like tents which in no way resembled the actual clothes which discreetly moulded breasts and thighs. I could not still my imagination. At night I lay in bed listening to Sister Emma moving quietly about her room next door. Boards creaked. Drawers thudded open and shut. A sash cord rattled in the casement. I plotted her movements, trying to guess when she stepped out of her dress, at what moment her stockings were peeled off, when she finally stood naked. There was alway a subdued shriek from the bed springs as she lay down, followed by a soft fluttering of the bed clothes as she composed herself for sleep. I felt like a spy but the intelligence I gathered was for my own delight. I did not want to share it.

In particular I did not want to tell Ray. He and Gladys had quarrelled, not for the first time but with a new conviction which invited everyone to take notice and take sides. It was not his fault, said Ray. Gladys was leaving the branch at the same time as Sadie and she had shown him letters from a former boy friend asking her to let him know when she was due to arrive in London.

'I can just see her tarting herself up to meet him,' he said bitterly.

'Is that what she said?'

'She doesn't need to say anything. I can tell.'

'How's that?'

'She kept his photograph. She said she'd torn it up, but I saw it in her diary.'

'What's he like?'

'Works in an office. Studies accountancy at evening classes.'

I could see that the would-be suitor offered serious competition. Accountancy, we were always being told, was a job with a future. It was frequently recommended by teachers as a career which would see us through from war to peace. Whatever the state of the world, accountants would always be needed. 'He probably earns a good bit,' I said.

'I expect so. Don't think Gladys hasn't thought of that.'

'Will she be there tonight?'

'I've not asked her. I don't care.'

The programme of the socials varied only a little from month to month. Sometimes there was a quiz, sometimes a sing-song. But always we ended up dancing to the radiogram. We sang as we danced, crooning into the ear of our partner: 'Amapola', 'All or Nothing at All', 'Jealousy'. We learned the words from song sheets sold by Woolworths, poring over them at meal-times and in the lavatory. Experts knew the verse as well as the chorus. Ray had been the first to memorise 'Deep Purple' from beginning to end. He sang it in the style of Bing Crosby, dredging up the deep notes from the bottom of his stomach and slitting his eyes as he warbled the high notes. Sister Joyce had once asked him to be quiet while they danced and he had not forgiven her.

The social was something to look forward to, expecially after a day in the potato field. Sadie was going; so was Sister Emma. We saw Mr King burrow under his pullover and cardigan to find the watch in his waistcoat pocket and we knew that deliverance was at hand. 'Last sacks,' he shouted and we piled them into the wagon waiting by the gate and climbed aboard. A few gulls followed us down the track, then heeled over on one wing and flew back to the meadow. It was only mid-afternoon but the light was going fast, soaking into the mist and broken earth. Winter was on its way. I could smell it in the dead leaves that filled the ditches. Christmas would be the dividing line. Sadie was going to London the following month and after that it was my birthday. I could not look forward without being elated and apprehensive at the same time.

I had a bath and washed my hair, then lay on my bed and read the *Saint Omnibus* that I had at last succeeded in borrowing from Darwen Library, two months after I had filled in the reservation card. Sister Emma put her head round the door. 'Are you going to take me to the social?'

'If you like.'

'You don't have to sound so enthusiastic.'

'I'm sorry.' Privately I was worried what the others might say if I arrived with a personal chaperone, but it would look obvious and rude if I went on my own. 'I wasn't thinking,' I said. 'I'd like to take you.'

She took my arm as we walked to the assembly hall and I was glad that it was dark. 'How's the fox-trot coming on?' she asked.

'I still can't reverse.'

'I'll show you.' She placed one hand around my waist and the other on my shoulder and steered me backwards down the road. I tripped on a pebble and clung to her for support. 'Careful,' she said, 'you'll have us over.' She let go of my shoulder and took my hand. 'Start on the beat,' she said, giving it a squeeze. 'Now! Slow, slow, quick-quick, slow. You see, it's easy.'

When we entered the hall Gladys Fisher whispered something to Sadie who blushed and covered her mouth with her handkerchief. I crossed the floor and drew her to the wall. 'What's so funny?'

'You and your nanny.'

'D'you think I need one? It's you who needs looking after.'

She drew back her head and looked at me down her nose. 'D'you think you're the one who can do it?'

'No one better.'

Sadie tucked her handkerchief up her sleeve and addressed the room at large. 'Fancies himself, doesn't he.'

The back-chat was an accepted ritual, but it was becoming increasingly boring. It was like running on the spot before setting off in the hundred yards sprint. The result of the race was not in doubt but we could not avoid the warm-up.

'East of the sun, West of the moon,' sang Frank Sinatra on the radiogram and Sadie tugged me on to the floor. I reversed as Sister Emma had taught me and over Sadie's shoulder I saw her nod approval.

'You're getting better,' said Sadie.

'I've been practising.'

It was one of my favourite records. I loved the soft, punchy arrangement and how the band swapped chorus and answer with the singer. 'They've got *Orchestra Wives* on at Bolton next week,' said Sadie. 'Can you come?'

'I'll try.' Glenn Miller was another of our favourites and his film was one we all wanted to see. It was not just the music of the bands that we admired but how they looked, sleek as sharks in their tuxedos, impossibly sophisticated, speaking a light and slangy patois that we tried to imitate. It was the language of hot dogs and highballs and cigarettes with half-inch filters. We did not understand it completely but we yearned to make it our own. Earlier that year a Canadian soldier who had been brought up in the Homes spent three days of his leave at Franklin House. Roddy James was moved elsewhere and for three night the soldier shared my room, stretched out on the bed, stripped to his vest and chain-smoking until the tin he used as an ashtray overflowed with dog-ends. When he returned to his unit he gave me a carton of Sweet Caporal. I hoarded them for as long as I could, rationing myself to one cigarette a day, and when the last packet was empty I pressed it in my copy of John Masefield. Canada was less exciting than America, but it was half-way there.

The social ended at ten o'clock. We successfully outvoted an attempt by Sister Agnes to turn the evening into a Beetle Drive. There was lemonade as well as orange squash at the soft drinks table and Ray made it up with Gladys Fisher. The last record was a waltz. 'Who's Taking You Home Tonight?'. Sadie pressed her cheek against mine and we circled the floor, holding each other as closely as we dared. We said goodnight at the door where Sister Agnes, now in charge of Argyle House, stood on guard, marshalling her flock behind her.

'Straight off home, Raymond Clutton,' she said. 'I don't want you sneaking round the cloakroom.'

He widened his eyes in mock astonishment. 'Me, Sister?'

The girls giggled and behind Sister Agnes's back, Gladys Fisher blew him a kiss. 'She's promised she won't see the other bloke,' he told me as we walked up the road with Sister Emma a few paces ahead.

'Do you believe her?'

'Why shouldn't I? We'll all be gone from here soon. There's no sense in making things awkward.'

'I suppose you're right.' I thought it unlikely that Gladys would keep her promise. I could not be sure of Sadie either but I was strangely unconcerned. Her imminent departure for London had driven us to a frenzy of vows, but they were as much a part of the pattern as our declarations of love which we plonked down like cards in a game of Snap. The chances were that I would not see her for a year; perhaps longer. But although there was little doubt I would miss her I could not pretend – at least to myself – that the loss would be unbearable. Separation was like a journey. Eventually it came to an end and I looked forward not only to our reunion, but what I might discover on the way.

Christmas came and went. On the Christmas shopping expedition to Bolton, a branch tradition which was also an opportunity for plunder, Skelly was arrested for shoplifting and Mr Rome was telephoned by the police to come and collect him. We saw him arrive back at the branch, white-faced in the back of Mr Rome's car and when we met later in the furnace room at Mosscrop he told us how the manager of the shop had threatened to take him to court.

'Old Rome told him he'd be putting the Homes in the dock and he let me go,' said Skelly.

'Jammy bugger,' said Ray. 'Did he give you a whacking?'

'Six on the arse.'

'Did it hurt?'

'Not like Buller's did. He kept telling me how I'd let him down. I thought he was going to cry.'

'What were you trying to pinch?' asked Doss.

Skelly felt in his jacket pocket and brought out a fountain pen. 'This. The manager left it on his desk and I nicked it when Rome took me back.'

'They'll bloody kill you if they find out,' said Ray.

Skelly felt in his other pocket and produced an ashtray. 'I got this too.'

We stared at him in admiration. He was quite mad, I thought. But his nerve was extraordinary. I remembered him looting Mr King's money bag. The risks he ran were nothing compared to the satisfaction he derived from robbing those who thought they had him under their control.

On Christmas Day we attended morning service in the village chapel and came back to a lunch of roast pork, followed by Christmas pudding and mince pies. In the afternoon we went for a walk. It was a day of high winds and brilliant sunshine. From the top of the moor we looked down on the Homes. Each roof shone as if it had been polished. Smoke streamed from every chimney. Trees bent low to the ground. Grass rippled and the water of the reservoir was chopped into neat white waves. The world was in motion. We sat in a hollow out of the wind and watched clouds scud over us, each one dissolving before it reached the railway viaduct. We seemed to be travelling backwards, sucked into the side of the hill where the bones and armour of those long-dead knights nourished the heather.

Gladys had wheedled the key of the laundry from one of the girls who worked there and she and Ray had arranged a meeting about which I was sworn to secrecy. 'It's just the two of us,' said Ray. 'Most likely it's the last time.' I thought of them in the Christmas calm, surrounded by mountains of white sheets, with all the machines still and no one to interrupt them. I wished them joy, but I envied them.

Sadie was in bed with a cold. I had given my present – an address book bound in morocco leather – to Gladys to deliver and received mine in return. It was a wallet with my initials stamped in gold across one corner. Sister Emma had given me a notebook, also leather-bound, in which to copy the best of the poems I was trying to write and I had given her a bottle of Yardley's cologne. My mother had sent me a book token and I had bought her a framed print by Rowland Hilder which showed a team of horses ploughing against a line of elms. Taken all round, honours seemed even.

Half a dozen of us had left the branch together on the walk, but Harry Barnes and I abandoned the others and climbed the steep path which cut diagonally across the face of the moor. He sat now with his hands locked around his knees, gazing towards Darwen as if projecting himself there. 'It's not for long,' I said.

'It's three weeks.'

'Two and a half.'

'Not counting weekends,' he said.

I had not seen Doreen again since our first meeting, but Harry continued to meet Fiona most days after school. Sometimes he played truant and they went to the cinema, occupying one of the loges at the back which the manager reserved for courting couples. Each one contained two double seats, not long enough to lie down on but sufficiently roomy for two people to recline at an angle, with their feet still on the floor. I went with them once to see *Blues in the Night* which featured the Will Bradley band, but Harry and Fiona were less interested in the film than in their own performance. After fifteen minutes I left them and found a seat in the main hall.

'Was it a good picture?' Harry asked me on our way home.

'I don't know why you bother going.'

'Yes you do.'

I could not dissemble with Harry. He believed most people's motives to be unworthy and gave himself credit for nothing, except honesty about his own obsession. I had never met anyone so single-minded. He did not claim to love Fiona, or she him. As he had told me after their first encounter, they did not have to talk. They were not interested in conversation. 'Straight at it,' he had said and seeing them together I believed him. He was a year older than me and in six months' time he would be sitting for his final examinations.

'How d'you think you'll do?' I asked him.

He turned both his thumbs down. 'Not a chance.'

'Don't you care?'

'Not a bit.'

'What will you do then?'

He plucked a blade of grass and squinted down the barrel towards the Victoria Tower, miles across the moor. 'It doesn't matter. It's not worth thinking about a proper job. I'll be called up soon. I'll find something to earn a few bob. I might as well enjoy myself.'

'What about Fiona?'

Harry laughed. 'It's not her real name, you know. That was just for starters. She's called Maggie.'

'And Doreen?'

'That's her cousin. Her real name's Lois. She's going to get married. She's asked Maggie to be a bridesmaid. Bloody silly thing to do. Who wants to settle down?'

'Lot's of people do.'

'Not me. Or you. Not if you think about it.' He pointed to the houses far below where people sat digesting their Christmas lunch. 'That's what they want you to do. Clock in, clock out. Be a good lad. Say "I will" and everybody's happy.' He heaved an enormous sigh as if he was expelling germs so noxious that they would poison him. 'They're not going to get me like that. All you have to do is not care. Go your own way. Let them say what they like.'

'What about your family?'

'What family? My father's dead and my mother's working in some bloody factory. Earning a packet. I've not heard from her for a year. She'll be glad to be shut of me.'

I thought of my own mother and the loyalty she preached. The bleakness of Harry's pronouncements was shocking, but it was their finality, the way in which they closed doors once and for all, which raised the hairs on the back of my neck.

'You're not really stuck on that Sadie, are you?' he asked.

'Quite.'

'So long as it's only quite.' He stood up and the wind instantly blew his hair over his face. 'Just get what you can,' he advised. 'Forget about the rest.'

A week later Sadie and Gladys travelled down to London. We had said our goodbyes the night before, shuddering in the cold outside the back door of Argyle House, and our public parting under the gaze of Sister Agnes was polite and restrained. Mr Rome was driving them to Bolton where they would catch the train to Manchester. It was the Northern Flier, travelling south.

'I'll write,' said Sadie.

'So will I.'

'You can give her a kiss,' said Sister Agnes and obediently I pecked her on the lips. She was wearing a two-piece costume in chocolate brown, with a shiny pink blouse gathered tightly at the throat. The colours did not suit her, nor did the coat she carried over her arm with its collar of imitation fur.

She showed me the locket about her neck. My photograph was inside it and I imagined the tiny black and white image of myself travelling between her breasts to a place I had never seen. 'Time to be off,' said Mr Rome and I kissed her again. Suddenly there seemed so much to say, but it was too late. Sister Agnes elbowed me to one side and the car drove away. We waved until it turned the bend in the road and as it disappeared from view we heard Mr Rome salute the school bus with his horn as it passed him on its way to collect us.

'Right you are then,' said Sister Agnes. 'That's that.'

'That's that,' repeated Harry and pushed me towards the bus stop.

What was extraordinary was the sense of relief. It did not come immeadiatley but in the following weeks I felt lighter, free of obligations. There was no one to whom I had to repeat the formulae which had grown so stale. Sadie and I exchanged letters in which at least half the final page comprised the familiar listings, but I found my eye skipping over words I already knew by heart. If I was feeling lonely or depressed I could turn to them for consolation, but I could obtain the same relief by reading a book or, even better, by seeing a film. They were all ways of filling in the time.

It was not Sadie's mind that I missed but her body. I dreamed about her constantly. I awoke with an erection which persisted throughout the day, materialising without warning in the middle of a biology class or in the gym as I was waiting my turn to vault the horse. I masturbated often and then fretted about feeling tired.

'Don't worry so much,' said Harry when I told him of my anxiety. 'You won't go blind.'

I concentrated on work; reading late into the night, learning poems. I had no appetite and lost weight. One day during a history lesson I fainted and awoke in Mr Gaskell's study. Chalk dust silted down from his hair as he bent over me. 'Feeling better?'

'Yes thank you, sir.'

'Been overdoing it a bit?'

'Yes sir, a bit.'

'Not worried about anything?'

'Not really, sir.'

He looked unconvinced. 'I want the doctor to have a look at you. Can't have you fainting all over the place. Very untidy.'

I realised that he had made a joke and tried to laugh. Instead, I found tears streaming down my face. I did not know why. I was not unhappy. I felt an overwhelming fatigue as though every tendon and nerve had been stretched like a length of elastic and then let go. I longed for sleep, but my body buzzed like a faulty soda siphon. I closed my eyes and saw the bubbles fizzing through my veins, one following another in endless succession.

Mr Gaskell gave me his handkerchief. 'Can you tell me what's wrong?'

'Nothing really, sir.'

'You don't cry about nothing.'

I sniffed miserably. I was tempted to invent a reason to satisfy him, but I found it hard to frame a coherent sentence.

'We'll see what the doctor thinks.' Mr Gaskell strode to his telephone and gave the necessary instructions. 'Swift's the word and prompt the action,' he said. It was an expression my mother sometimes used and, without warning, the tears welled up once more.

The doctor diagnosed strain and ordered me to spend a week in bed. Yet again Sister Emma moved Roddy James next door so that I could have the room to myself, but I was

still on edge. I slept badly and dozed on until mid-morning.
For some time I could not think where I was or what I was
doing there. It was the first time I had been in the house on a
weekday and I felt isolated, marooned almost, as though I
had been put ashore while the business of the day steamed
on and conducted itself elsewhere.

Sister Emma put her head round the door. 'Would you
like some coffee?'

'I'd love some.'

She backed in with the tray and sat on my bed. 'Mind
your feet.' She made herself comfortable, settling into the
bedclothes like a hen squirming down on a clutch of eggs,
and when she saw me smiling she wagged her finger. 'It's
no good you looking so pleased with yourself. You gave us
a proper scare.'

'I'm sorry.'

'What got into you?'

'I just felt rotten. It's been getting worse all term.'

She tasted her coffee and added another spoonful of
sugar. 'I shouldn't' she said. 'But I will.' She took another
sip and smacked her lips. 'Why didn't you say something?
You can surely talk to me.'

'About most things,' I said.

'What does that mean?'

'I didn't know what to talk about. I didn't know what was
wrong. I don't know now.'

'Are you sure?'

I thought of the dreams and my creaking bed which I felt
sure she must have heard through the wall. 'Certain.'

She studied me for a long time. 'I wonder.'

'You wonder what?'

'I wonder if you're telling me the truth.'

'Of course I am.' I felt my face start to glow. 'It's hot in
here,' I said.

'Is that all?' She put down her cup and opened a window.
When she reached upwards to loosen the catch I could see
dimples at the back of her knees. I did not want her to go
away. She was easier to talk to than Sadie had ever been.

'Why did you come here in the first place?' I asked.

'That's too long a story.'

'Didn't you want to get married?'

'Most people do at one time or another. I still might.'

'What about children?'

'What about them? You want to know too much. Anyway, I've got a houseful.'

'It's not the same as having your own.'

'Isn't it?' she said. 'And how would you know?'

She stooped to pick up the tray and I smelled her body, a sweet rush of scent that billowed from the open neck of her dress. It was a clean domestic smell like baking or lavender polish. I put my hand on her arm. 'Can't you stay?'

'I mustn't. I've got things to do.'

'But you'll come back.'

'When I have time.'

She visited me again in the afternoon and in the evening when she was seeing the rest of the boys to bed. 'Do you want your window left open?' she asked.

'All the way.'

It was early summer and a heat wave was forecast. That night I took off my pyjamas and lay with only the sheet covering me. It was too hot to sleep. I draped the shade of my bedside lamp with a coloured handkerchief and read thrillers until my eyes felt heavy. I did not own a watch but I could hear the church clock in the village chiming the hours. At two o'clock the door opened. 'I saw your light,' said Sister Emma. 'Are you all right?'

'I just can't sleep.'

'You must try.'

'It's so hot,' I said. 'I could do with a swim.'

She smiled and shook her head. 'We'll try something else.'

She went away and returned with a bowl of lukewarm water and a sponge. 'This will cool you,' she said. She dabbed the sponge lightly over my face and forehead. 'Is that better?'

'Much.'

She folded back the sheet and sponged my chest. My skin erupted into goose-pimples and I shivered. 'Not too cold?'

I shook my head and she pulled the sheet down an inch or two more, but I hung on to it. 'I've got nothing on.'

'Then you can do the rest yourself,' she said. She put the palm of her hand against my cheek, first on one side then the other. 'I think you're cooler already.'

'I am.'

'Try and sleep then.' She went out quietly, closing the door behind her.

I got out of bed and sponged myself from head to toe but I was still burning. I drew the curtains and looked out on to the road winding between dry-stone walls. Moonlight frosted the moors. Owls cried, hunting up and down the valley and from somewhere near the station there was the chink and rumble of rolling stock being shunted along the line. I thought of Sadie far away in London and I was wrenched by a longing so intense that it made me catch my breath. I walked through the adjoining room, between the rows of iron cots and into the corridor where I paused outside Sister Emma's door. I opened it and saw her standing by the window as if she had been waiting for me. She was naked and as she turned her breasts, her belly and her thighs were rimed with silver. I put my arms round her and felt her shudder and when we kissed she breathed into my mouth and it was a sound of welcome and despair.

I pushed her back on to the bed, kneeling between thighs that hemmed me in like boulders, shoving eagerly and clumsily to root myself inside her. She raised her hips and let me in. For a moment I lay still, the blood dinning in my ears. Slowly and carefully she locked our ankles and held me fast. When we moved, we moved together. I was floating on dry land, buried in air, soaring and exploding and spiralling over and over like a leaf into darkness. I felt sweat dewing my back. 'I love you,' I said and she kissed me and said 'Now you can go back to sleep.'

Her arms were round me, my head was cushioned on her

breasts and I knew she would tell me anything. 'How old are you?' I asked.

She hesitated. 'Does it matter?'

'I just wanted to know.'

'I'm thirty,' said Emma.

Twice my age, I thought. 'I wish I was thirty,' I said and then I slept until she woke me three hours later, when I crept back to my own bed to sleep again. For a while I lay awake. I felt happy and fearful and amazed. Nothing I had heard or imagined had warned me it would be like this. It was not only different but better than I had expected. And it was so simple. Anyone could do it and they could go on doing it daily, nightly, without permission, for ever and ever. I closed my eyes and fell into dreams of eternity.

Eleven

WHEN I AWOKE the house was silent. The boys had gone to school or to work and sunlight streamed through the windows on to their empty beds. It was hard to believe what had happened only a few hours earlier. I felt so altered that when I took off my pyjamas and examined my body I looked for evidence of change, printed like a transfer on the skin. It was almost disappointing to find myself unmarked. I washed and dressed and went downstairs to find Emma alone in the kitchen. She did not hear me enter the room and I crept behind her and put my arms about her waist.

She spun round. 'Don't do that!'

'Why not?' I thought she was joking and held on but she broke my grip and thrust me away.

'Don't ever do that,' she said. 'Keep your hands to yourself. I don't like being mauled.'

'I wasn't mauling you.'

'That's what it looked like. What if someone had come in? What if Sister Kathleen had seen?' Her face was flushed and she was out of breath. 'What happened last night was wrong. It can't happen again.'

'You wanted it to happen.'

'That's beside the point. It was wrong. Can't you see that?'

I shook my head and she stepped towards me, her hands raised as if she intended to shake sense into me. 'You must put it from your mind.'

'It's too late for that,' I said.

'You must try.'

I could not understand what had gone wrong. The night before there had been no debate, no equivocation. What had happened had been extraordinary but it had followed a kind of logic engaging bodies, if not minds. I had not for a moment considered whether what we were doing was good or bad. It did not concern me. Nor, it occurred to me, had it worried Emma at the time. Her change of heart was too sudden for me to believe.

'Nobody knows,' I said. 'Nobody's going to know.'

'That's not the point,' she said again. 'What's important is that it has to stop. Now. This instant. We have to forget about it.'

'I can't do that.'

'You must.'

'But it was wonderful,' I said. 'I'll never forget it.'

She gave a cry that was half anger, half exasperation and with one hand swept a pile of plates into the sink. I saw the splinters fly and fall to the floor and methodically she began to pick them up. I knelt down to help her and our foreheads bumped as gently as two balloons. She rested her arms on my shoulders and held me captive. 'It's my fault,' she said. 'I'm to blame.'

'No you're not.'

'How would you know. Fifteen years old. I'm responsible. I'm supposed to be in charge.'

Her breath was hot on my neck. I stroked her back and felt my fingers catch against the frail harness of underwear beneath her dress. She stirred against my hand and I stroked harder. 'No,' said Emma. 'Not again.' She stood up quickly and I overbalanced. 'You'll have to go away,' she said. 'I shall speak to Mr Rome. You'll have to go to another house.'

'What will you tell him?'

'I'll think of something.'

I lay back and looked at her. 'No you won't.'

'Don't sound so smug,' said Emma. 'Who do you think you are? Who do you think you're talking to?'

I caught something of her desperation. 'You,' I said. 'The one who made love to me.' It was unfair. I was using secret knowledge. I had seen her naked and it gave me power if not authority. I saw her wince but I was beyond caring. I wanted the revelations to continue. I would do anything to defend them. 'I love you,' I said.

She smoothed her dress over her hips and drew a deep breath. 'You're too young to know about love.'

'Teach me.'

'I can't do that,' said Emma. 'You have to find out for yourself.'

'Help me up then.'

She pulled me to my feet and turned me about face. 'No more talk. But I mean what I say. It can't happen again.'

I had breakfast and went out. The doctor had given me a week's convalescence and I was absolved from work. As I walked up the road I met the cows wending their way back to their meadow after milking. They stirred eddies of their own grassy breath as they ambled past, their haunches patched with dung. The previous year I had tried to ride one of them, lowering myself on to its back as it stood in the shippon. But it had bucked and capered so that I had to haul myself back on to the beam away from its horns. I could not remember which cow I had chosen as my mount, but they all seemed to look at me warily as they slouched through the gate and into the meadow. Doss waved at me from the entrance to the farm and I followed him across the road into the dairy.

It had white tiled walls and a red tile floor. There were churns in one corner and the cooler stood in another. 'Give us a hand,' said Doss and I helped him lift the big bucket of milk and pour it into the drum on the top of the cooler. The milk flowed over a corrugated steel panel and through a strainer into another bucket below. After each pouring the strainer was rinsed free of hairs and dirt.

It was a simple job and a reasonably pleasant one, but one had to take care in pouring the milk. The bucket was heavy and it was hard to prevent milk slopping over the brim. After three trips to the cooler whoever was pouring had a soaked jacket which smelled sour at the end of the day. By the end of the week it was offensive to wear. Sister Beryl insisted on Doss keeping his milking jacket at the farm.

'What are you doing home then?'

'I had a funny turn at school. I fainted.'

He looked impressed. 'Go on.'

'Strain, the doctor said.'

'There's plenty of that around here.'

I tapped my forehead. 'Mental strain. They say I've been studying too hard.'

Doss looked sceptical but said nothing. Working on the farm had filled him out. His shoulders were broader than mine and his face seemed to have widened. He had a sweet and uncomplaining temper, but he was also stubborn. He would listen to the arguments, but once he had made up his mind it was hard to change it. We had all tried to talk him out of working on the farm, but he would not be dissuaded.

'But it's not scientific,' Ray told him.

'I don't mind about that. I want to work with stock.'

'There's diseases you can get from animals,' said Skelly.

'Such as?'

'Ringworm for a start. I knew a lad had to have his head shaved.'

'I expect he managed,' said Doss.

When two of the boys had taken Mr Cobb's son to the pig-sty and filled his boots with pig shit, telling him that manure would make him grow taller just as it did the beans in the vegetable garden, it was Doss who led him to the tap and washed his boots out. I wished that I could talk to him about Sister Emma, but he did not have a girl friend as far as I knew and while I knew that he would be interested, I thought he might also be shocked. I did not want to give either of us uninvited problems.

I helped him with the mucking out. The shippons were awash with liquid manure which he brushed from the stalls into the central gulley, sweeping it in a khaki tide towards a barrow by the door. The barrow was too unwieldy for me to manage, but Doss wheeled it across the cobbled yard, the manure slopping over his hands like thin porridge, up the ramp and on to the midden. There were potholes and lengths of chain to avoid and he treated the job as an obstacle race, with only himself to beat.

'Mr Jackson says I've got the makings of a farmer,' he said.

'Only the makings?'

'That's to be going on with. He says I should take it up.'

I thought of Mr Jackson's dead son, but said nothing. It was not my story to tell. 'After you leave here, you mean?'

'That's right. Not at another farm though. At college. He says he can help.'

'You should let him.'

Doss propped the barrow against the wall. 'I reckon I will. He says it's not only a good job, but it might save me from getting killed. I can farm instead of getting called up.'

'Is that what you want?'

'I don't see why not.' Doss rubbed the manure from his hands with a piece of sacking. 'When old Buller was talking about the war effort I never thought much of it. Piss and wind like everything else, I reckon.'

'That was just Buller.'

'D'you think Rome's any better?'

'Lots,' I said.

'I'm not so sure. He gives us things but he expects more. You should know. He's got his eye on you.'

It was true, I thought, and I experienced a sudden queasiness as I imagined what he would say if he knew what had happened with Emma.

'I reckon he's soft on those Sisters at Franklin,' said Doss.

'Why d'you say that?'

'He's always round there. You should hear old Pod go on about it. In and out, in and out. Mr Rome's home from home.'

My nausea was replaced by a surge of jealousy, as violent as it was unexpected. 'Don't be daft.'

'I'm only telling you what she says.'

'It's just gossip.'

'They're all saying it.' He picked at his nails with their khaki rims. 'Who cares anyhow?'

It was not true, I told myself as I left the farm. Sister

Beryl's spite would distort her view of anything she thought was unusual. But there was no doubt that Mr Rome was a constant visitor to Franklin House. Many a time I had gone into the sitting room to find him there, rocking in front of the fire, while Emma sat in her usual chair, her shins rosy in the glow of the coals. I always sensed I was interrupting something, not necessarily a conversation, but a dialogue which was felt rather than spoken.

Was it possible that Emma was telling me to stay away because she was already involved with Mr Rome? It was so unlikely that my instinct was to dismiss the idea without further consideration. But that evening I was called to the sitting room to report to him on how I was feeling and seeing him in the chair next to Emma, tapping her knee to emphasise some point he was making, pausing only briefly in mid-sentence to wave me in, my suspicions flared again.

'Up and about, I see,' he said.

'Yes sir.'

'Not making a nuisance of yourself, I hope.'

'Of course he's not,' said Emma.

'I've been out all day,' I said. 'Sister doesn't want me hanging around.'

My tone was surly and Mr Rome frowned. 'Sister Emma has a great deal to do. So does Sister Kathleen. You can't expect them to be at your beck and call.'

'No sir.'

'You don't sound convinced.' He turned to Emma. 'Is there anything wrong?'

'Not that I know of.'

Liar, I thought. 'Sister Emma said I was talking too much,' I said. 'She told me I needed to clear my mind.'

'Excellent advice,' said Mr Rome. 'And did you take it?'

'I've been walking,' I said. 'Taking exercise. I'll do the same tomorrow. I don't want to be underfoot.'

He stretched his legs towards the empty grate. 'I don't suppose any of us do. Very well then. Off you go. Come and see me at the end of the week.' He turned to Emma.

'You'll see he does that, Sister? So that we can give him a clean bill of health.'

Emma looked me up and down. 'I'm sure he won't need reminding. He has an excellent memory.'

She avoided me for the rest of the evening and at night her door was locked. The next night was the same, but instead of padding back to my bed I rattled the doorknob backwards and forwards until she came to the other side. 'Go away,' hissed Emma. 'You'll wake the house.'

'I want to talk to you.'

'Not now.'

'Just for a minute.'

'You'll wake Sister Kathleen.'

I rattled more loudly and drummed on the door with my fingertips until it opened half an inch.

'What is it you want?'

'To see you.' I put my shoulder to the door but she held it firm. 'Sister Kathleen's coming,' I said. 'She just put her light on.'

Instantly Emma pulled me into her room and closed the door behind me. 'Are you sure?'

'Not really.' I sat on the edge of the bed, well pleased with myself.

'It's not funny.'

'I never said it was.' I had a feeling that if I could maintain a dialogue, however foolish or fractious, it would serve in the same way as the back-chat between Sadie and me, granting us time to lay foundations on which to manoeuvre.

'You can't stay,' said Emma.

'I wanted to say I was sorry. I was rude.'

'You certainly were.'

'I heard something about you and Mr Rome. That he was soft on you.'

She snorted impatiently. 'Branch gossip. No one in their right mind believes that.'

'It worried me. It made me jealous.'

She did not reply and I pressed my advantage. 'I've

missed you.'

'I can't help that. You've got to go now.'

'Have you missed me?'

She tugged at the cord of her dressing gown as if she was securing a parcel. 'Of course I've missed you. Is that what you want to hear?'

'If it's true.'

'You know it's true,' said Emma. 'You're not a fool. You know what you're doing.'

'That's not what you said.'

'I was wrong.'

I took her hands and pulled her towards the bed. 'Come and lie down.'

'No.'

'Just for a minute.'

'That's what you said when I let you in. Your minute's up.'

'Starting now.' I picked at the cord and the dressing gown swung open. 'Please,' I said. My strategy was at an end. I wanted nothing more in the world than to be between the sheets with Emma. I wanted to be buried inside her, walled by flesh. It was my only ambition. I could hear myself yelling it silently. I could not think beyond it.

She rested on one elbow. 'You'll go when I say?'

I nodded. I was willing to promise anything. I would have cut off my hand if she had made it a condition for staying.

'For a little while then.' She stretched out beside me and I reached for her, steadily at first and then with a scrambling, reckless greed that shook the breath out of me. I snapped off the bedside light and we wrestled in the dark. She fought me like an enemy, almost throwing me to the floor. Her head thrashed from side to side as she avoided my mouth, but when we kissed her body seemed to soften and melt. I hung over her and drove into her and I felt as though I was performing an exorcism, ridding myself of ghosts, worshipping and exulting and receiving absolution. It was different from the first time. I was not being comforted. I was fighting and winning. But there remained a pocket of sense, lodged somewhere at the back of my skull, which uttered a faint but persistant signal like a transmitter buried in a bunker far below the battlefield. You are not responsible, it said. You are not to blame.

The wind blew the curtains apart and in the moonlight I saw us beached side by side in a shipwreck of blankets. I licked my arm and it tasted of salt. 'This can't go on,' said Emma.

It was as though nothing had happened and she was simply resuming the conversation we had begun in the kitchen two days previously.

'I mean it,' she said. 'Life will be impossible.'

I ran my finger across her damp stomach and felt it quake as though I had touched her funny-bone. 'What will be impossible?'

'The lies. The pretence. Someone's bound to notice.'

'I don't see why.'

'You don't want to see why.'

The curtains billowed out into the room and when she got up to shut the window I followed her and stroked her shoulders and breasts. 'It's all right,' I said. 'Don't worry.'

She stamped her foot in slow motion. 'Don't be foolish. Just go to bed.' She turned round and kissed me briefly on the mouth. 'Go on. Before any more's said. Just go.'

'You won't keep me out?'

'We'll see.'

'You won't keep me out,' I said.

Roddy James woke as I was about to climb into my own bed. I tucked him in and combed his hair with my fingers. 'Where've you been?' he complained.

'Nowhere.'

'I woke up and you weren't here.'

'No you didn't. I've been here all the time.'

'You weren't here,' he repeated. 'I was going to come and look for you.'

'What about the crocodiles?' Roddy believed that, after dark, crocodiles swarmed under his bed. His mother had invented the story to keep him in his room while she went out drinking.

'You told me there weren't any.'

'They might come back,' I said. 'You can't be too careful.'

Emma was right, I thought. Someone was bound to notice, but there was a gulf between what they saw and what they understood which reduced the risk. What I failed to see then was how tempting it would become to shorten the odds. I could not tell anyone about Emma and myself. But part of me wanted to scatter clues and drop hints that something momentous had happened which made me wiser, more worldly than my friends. I wanted to impress Sister Kathleen too and at breakfast-time, only a few hours after I had crept past her door, I would contrive to mention how I had heard the farm dogs barking before dawn or how the house creaked on its timbers at night, so that she would ask what had kept me awake and how long it had been before I went back to sleep, and without her realising quite how or why it happened I was identified in her mind as a prowler, a keeper of secrets, knowing more than I was prepared to say.

Emma was not pleased. 'You create problems,' she said. 'Kathleen knows something's wrong. The questions she asks. I feel so deceitful.'

'Why don't you tell her?'

'I think you'd like that,' said Emma.

'I wouldn't mind.'

'Well, I can't. I wouldn't know how to explain it. I feel so ashamed.'

'What of?'

'Not what you think. There's nothing wrong in making love, not that I can see. But it's wrong for you and me. We insult people when we deceive them. It makes them look fools. And it's only because they trust us. It isn't fair.'

I could see what she meant, but I would not accept her argument. 'How would you feel about telling that girl in London?' she asked. 'What do you think she'd say?'

'That's different,' I said.

'Isn't it just,' said Emma.

Sadie continued to write to me every week and in Franklin House my letters now came to me unopened. I replied less regularly, not only because I could not truthfully describe the important changes in my life but because everything outside them seemed drab and uneventful compared to her life in London. She saw films long before they crept north on general release. She went dancing at Hammersmith Palais. She had a job as a secretary. She sent me photographs of herself sitting in Hyde Park but she did not say who the photographer was who had made her smile so unaffectedly. When I demanded to know she ignored the question as though it was irrelevant.

'She doesn't have to account to you,' said Emma.

'What do you know about it?'

'You're being rude again. Don't speak to me like that.'

Sharing Emma's bed once or twice a week had made us familiars, but the affection in which we had held each other was chafed by subterfuge and suspicions. The old relationship between house mother and charge was gone and could never be restored. But for the benefit of the watchers like Sister Beryl its semblance had to be maintained. The pretence aggravated us both. It made me insolent and Emma defensive. I knew she would not report my bad manners to Mr Rome and each day I provoked her more and more. Our arguments became quarrels and making love did not end them, but only increased the irritation. We had formed a habit which neither of us was able to break. We turned to each other for comfort and were dispirited when we did not find it.

In the late summer we heard that a psychologist was visiting the branch to make an assessment of the older boys and girls. Her name was Polly Millman and she and Sister Kathleen had been together at college. 'So she'll be staying at Franklin,' Emma told me.

'What's she like?'

'Shrewd. We can't see each other while she's here. Not much escapes Polly.'

I was intrigued rather than put out. I had never met a psychologist before but in films they were figures of enlightenment, tilting at institutions in a way which struck me as exemplary. Polly, as she insisted on being called, did not match the image. She was blond and rakish and cynical, but it soon became clear that she viewed institutions not as her natural quarry but as potential employers. She had just completed a year in a munitions factory where she had advised on industrial relations. 'Awfully thick, those women,' she said. 'They can't strike. It's against the law. So they bitch, bitch, bitch all day long. Production simply goes downhill. There was that business with the milk. Somebody heard they were entitled to two free pints a day and they were only getting one, so they threatened to go slow. The management were tearing their hair. Help, they said. So help I did.'

'How?' I asked, certain that some professional mystery was about to be revealed.

'I told them to water it,' said Polly. 'Not letting on to the people on the shop floor, of course. They thought they were getting their proper ration. Honour was satisfied. Production went up. Simple.' She spread her hands and smiled as though she had just pulled a rabbit from a hat.

'You mean to say nobody twigged it?'

'Absolutely not,' she said. 'I told you, they're not awfully bright.'

For a month Polly became part of our lives. She talked to us individually and in groups. She joined us on walks. She occupied the sitting room, tapping out her notes on a portable typewriter. 'I'm in your way,' she said when I called in one day looking for a book.

'No you're not.'

'Come and sit down,' she said, slapping the seat of the armchair. 'Tell me what you've been doing.'

'Nothing much.'

'What's happening with that business of missing

physics?'

'We're sorting it out,' I said.

The double physics lesson on Friday morning was an enduring nightmare. The subject baffled and frightened me. It was worse than mathematics, more intractable than trigonometry. For six consecutive weeks I missed the train which got me to school in time for the class and each week my dilemma grew worse. I was now not only significantly behind the rest of the form, but my exercise book was blank and I knew it was only a matter of time before my truancy was discovered. The sooner I confessed, the sooner I would serve my sentence. But then I would be back on the physics treadmill, as miserable and mystified as I had been before.

The physics master was named Mr Cawston. He was a tall, sallow man whose sharp features and oily black hair looked as though they were being winched together tightly in a clamp at the base of his skull. He appeared to have been streamlined, an impression which would have pleased him had anyone dared to tell him. He was dedicated to science and could not tolerate anyone who denied its appeal. He said nothing about my regular absences until one day we passed each other in the corridor and his hand descended on my shoulder.

'We have not had the pleasure of your company for some time,' he said.

'I missed the train, sir.'

'Several trains,' said Mr Cawston, taking a diary from his pocket. 'Six in all. Tell me, does this misfortune occur on any other day of the week or is it confined to Fridays?'

'I don't know, sir.'

'There are many things you don't know,' said Mr Cawston, 'and with each lesson that you miss they multiply. Can you, for example, repeat Boyle's Law?'

It was the kind of interrogation I dreaded. 'No sir.'

'Boyle's Law,' said Mr Cawston, steering me along the corridor by his fingertips, 'states that at constant temperature the volume of a given mass of gas is inversely proportional to its pressure. Repeat that.'

I did so, with several mistakes. It made no sense to me whatever and I waited apprehensively for the next question. It was as bad as I had anticipated. 'What do you know of Avogadro's Law?' asked Mr Cawston.

'Nothing, sir.'

'Avogadro's Law,' he chanted, 'states that equal volumes of all gases under the same conditions of temperature and pressure contain the same number of molecules.' He let go of my shoulder and smiled thinly. 'Do you find that of interest?'

'Yes sir.'

'I doubt it, but the fact remains that the information is part of the teaching syllabus and I am obliged to make sure that you have absorbed it.' He consulted his diary once again. 'Today is Monday. The next physics lesson is on Friday. Between then and now you will copy every exercise that you have missed into your physics book. You will present it for my inspection and we will then discuss the matter further. Do you follow me?'

'Yes sir,' I said and he inclined his head.

'Consult the time-table,' he advised. 'We want no more missed trains.'

I borrowed Phil Watson's physics book and copied the exercises I had missed. It took me all week and I was no wiser at the end of it.

'When I leave school I shall never open another physics book,' I told Polly Millman.

'But you need it now to pass your School Certificate.'

'I'll manage without it.'

'Good English isn't enough on its own,' she said. 'Even journalists need to know more than composition.'

'We don't write composition. We write essays.' I did not believe that Polly Millman had any idea what journalists were required to know. Her loyalties were being made increasingly clear. When she recited the list of required subjects and necessary examinations I knew that she belonged to the Other Side. Precisely what it comprised and who its leaders and representatives were I was not certain. But, without doubt, they included the ones who – as Harry had perceived – only felt safe in a docile society in which all rules were followed, all regulations obeyed.

The weekend before Harry sat for his School Certificate I was sent for by Mr Rome. It was Friday evening and he was already wearing his leisure uniform of sports jacket and flannels. As always, his shoes gleamed like chestnuts. Even the laces had been waxed. 'Was Barnes on the train with you this afternoon?'

'No sir, I didn't see him. I think he was revising in the library.'

'Are you sure of that?'

'That's what he said he was going to do.'

Mr Rome stared at me, narrowing his eyes as if he could somehow drill down to a deeper layer of truth. 'Is he a close friend of yours?'

'Pretty close, sir.'

'Does he have friends in the town?'

'I think so, sir.' I began to guess what had happened, but decided it was more prudent to wait for Mr Rome to tell me.

'He's not reported back to his house,' he said. 'No one appears to have seen him since midday.' I said nothing and he shifted irritably in his chair. 'Have you no suggestion to make?'

'Have you spoken to the school, sir?'

'Of course I've spoken to the school. Where else could he be?'

'I don't know, sir.' There were so many places, I thought. There was the cinema, the derelict house, the moors; wherever he and Fiona used to meet. Over the past few weeks we had seen little of each other except on the journeys to and from school. But one day on the train he had reacted strangely to the story of my encounter with Mr Cawston.

'You're right about physics,' he said. 'It's all balls.' He took his own books from his satchel and without moving from his seat, tossed them, one by one, through the carriage window.

The train was half-way across the viaduct. Below us the lake glittered in the morning sun and moorhens jerked their way in and out of the reeds. Harry's books sailed through the air, their pages flapping like wings. We had travelled on before they hit the water.

'What did you do that for?'

'They're no more use to me,' he said.

'There's weeks to go yet.'

'I've finished,' said Harry. 'I'm doing no more.'

'What about the exams?'

'Sod the exams. I've no hope of passing. Why should I bother?' He lit a cigarette and smoked it reflectively, guarding the ash until it was at least an inch long.

'What will you do?'

'I've already told you. Earn a few bob till I'm called up. Don't look so worried. It's not the end of the world.' The train dived into a tunnel and as he drew on his cigarette the glow carved his face into its familiar Red Indian contours. His calm was not reassuring. It was like the composure of a man who had received the news of his impending death and decided to treat it with indifference. He would not appeal and he could not explain. I wondered if he was ever happy.

'If you know where he is or can suggest anywhere we might enquire it's your duty to tell me,' said Mr Rome.

'No idea, sir.'

He sighed, even more dolefully than usual. 'It's a serious matter. I shall have to inform the police.'

'Yes sir.'

'Very well then. If anything occurs to you, let me know.' He leaned forward across his desk. 'We should help him. We should help each other.'

Harry would not be impressed, I thought. I remembered the books sailing through the carriage window and the copper mask of his face. The best help I could give was to remain silent. Five days later he was found by the police in Blackpool. He was with Maggie who had been Fiona and they were caught stealing milk from a doorstep.

'Poor cow,' he said when, eventually, he was returned to the Homes. 'She doesn't even like milk. We had a good few days though. Until the money ran out.'

'How much did you have?' asked Spiff.

'Fifty quid.'

'Go on! Where did you get it?'

'Here and there.' He refused to specify but I thought of the shops whose tills we had plundered.

'Where did you stay?'

'In a boarding house. Double bed, gas fire.' He stretched himself and yawned luxuriously. 'We didn't get up at all the first day. Shagging non-stop.'

Spiff's jaw dropped. 'What was it like?'

'What do you mean what was it like?' Harry looked round the furnace room for inspiration. 'It's like that stove. It's all around you. You can feel yourself burning up but it never goes out. Not completely. You can always light it up again.'

I envied him. He made it sound so uncomplicated. 'What have they done with Fiona?' I asked.

'You mean Maggie. Her mother came to fetch her. She gave her a right telling off. Me as well.'

'What will she do?'

'It's up to her,' said Harry. 'She's her own boss. At least she will be soon.'

'Will you be seeing her again?'

'Not a chance. They're packing me off tomorrow.' He fluttered his fingers in mock farewell. 'I'm going to London. They're putting me in a hostel. At least, they think they are but I shan't stay there long. They'll be glad to be shut of me.' I must have looked apprehensive because he gripped my shoulder and shook it. 'I'm fed up with telling you: don't worry so much. It's not the end of the world. I'll look up Sadie for you if you like.'

'No thanks.'

'Don't you trust me? Quite right too.' Harry distributed the last of his cigarettes and we squatted around the furnace smoking them. Spiff collected the dog-ends and shredded them in his tobacco tin then, self-consciously, we all shook hands.

'All you have to do is not care,' said Harry. 'Remember that.'

He left the branch the next day wearing a new blue raincoat and carrying a suitcase made of compressed cardboard. One of its corners was already scuffed and a heel of yellow fibre poked through the skin of brown paint. Mr Rome pushed him into the car and slammed the door. Seeing us about to cross the road he waved us back. 'I don't want any of you talking to this boy,' he said. 'He's made quite enough mischief as it is. Just get on with your own business.' Harry grinned through the rear window as he drove away, the smile barely creasing his face. I wished we could have said goodbye, but it was difficult to know if he cared one way or the other.

Polly Millman also returned to London at the end of the week. She gave me a packet of razor blades as a parting gift. 'Don't cut yourself,' she said, 'and don't mess things up like your friend did.'

'I won't.'

'And don't give up on physics. Remember what I told you.'

I followed her to the front door and stacked her cases in the porch. 'What are you going to say about me in your report?'

'I don't know yet. I've not finished the assessment.'

'Will you send me a copy?'

'We'll see.'

She did not send it to me, but months later the girl who had followed Sadie into the branch office filched a copy from the files. It was in blue type on salmon-pink paper and it was headed Psychologist's Report. I slid it carefully into my pocket to read later in my room. 'Temperamentally he is likely to prove individualistic although sociable,' Polly had written.

> His scores on the two temperamental tests suggest that he is cheerful, natural and sociable, having a sense of humour, some adaptability and quickness of apprehension often amounting to jumping to conclusions. He also appears to be sensitive, feeling intensely, pleased by harmony in his surroundings, liking to develop ideas for their own sake, but impressed by only one idea at a time, rather effeminate, easily discouraged and careless of detail. His interests are likely to be in languages and the humanities rather than in science: a point made all too clear by his successive school reports. He falls into the category of 'rebel' and is likely to feel misunderstood and at times to be touchy and obstinate.

I felt vaguely complimented and also reassured. Polly's assessment of me was as shrewd as I had been warned to expect, but she had still failed to uncover the most important part of my life. She could file and index and categorise me but she did not know about Emma. The report stopped short of any important disclosure. I hid it between the pages of John Masefield and went downstairs, taking my secrets with me.

Twelve

HARRY WROTE to me a month later. Pinned to his letter and folded within a square of blue tissue paper was a £5 note. 'Hope they don't see this,' wrote Harry. 'It's to help keep you going till you get away. I did a bunk from the hostel where they took me and have got myself a job on the railways as a dining-car attendant. We're supposed to wash the plates between servings but we chuck half of them out of the window. Remember my school books? You can see where I got the idea.'

I took the letter with me to Sunday morning service and read it again and again until I knew the words by heart. There was no address. 'Most likely I'll be moving from where I am,' Harry explained. 'Besides which, I don't know who might cast their beady eyes over this and I don't want them to know where I'm staying. I will write again when I'm settled. Remember what I said. Don't let the bastards grind you. Abyssinia!'

I tried to visualise him somewhere in London; free of surveillance, free of responsibility. He made it sound exciting, even romantic. But by writing to me he had given himself a bearing; the place he had last been. It was his point of departure and I was still here to remind him what he had wanted to escape. I envied him but it sounded a restless and possibly lonely life. The world was so big that it was no wonder we tried to hold on to each other.

The minister announced the next hymn. It was 'Praise my soul, the King of heaven' and, as we sang, my eyes skipped down the page to the last verse. One line stood out and I stopped singing to read it silently to myself. When the congregation caught up with me I joined in.

Angels, help us to adore him;
Ye behold him face to face;
Sun and moon bow down before him,
Dwellers all in time and space;
Alleluiah! Alleluiah! Praise with us the God of grace.

We were all dwellers in time and space, I thought; Harry and my mother and Emma and Sadie, all joined through me, but each of us separate in our dispositions and desires. I saw us leaping or limping through infinity, the stars at our back and fathoms of air at our feet. When we travelled in pairs it was for fear of the dark; none of us wanted to be alone. But the partnerships were of necessity or for convenience. Nothing endured; there was no permanent shelter. Whatever the Bible promised, two people never truly became one flesh. The chapel shook with the thunder of the organ and I felt the pew in front of me vibrate beneath my hands. What the hymn so resoundingly affirmed I could not believe. We were not ransomed, or healed, or restored, or forgiven. We rejoiced only because we did not wish to be afraid.

Sadie wrote to me less frequently than when she first went away and her letters had changed. She was no longer excited by the novelty of London or if she was she concealed it, as though reluctant to spell out the attractions that awaited me. Often she sounded a warning note. Digs were difficult to find. Money did not go far. The blitz that week had been dreadful. My expectations were being damped down but I longed to go, as much for what I would be leaving as for what lay ahead. I was curiously untouched by stories of the bombing. Polly Millman had told us of standing at night on Hampstead Heath and watching London burn far below. But no one I knew had been killed. I responded only to the drama and understood none of the misery.

Like Harry I had begun to see the future as a series of short-term engagements which one experienced and then moved on. It meant travelling light, with few loyalties and no sense of continuity. I resented anyone who might get in the way or slow me down. My mother was maintaining her pressure on me to find work near home. Emma was writing to friends in London, seeking someone who might advise me how to address myself to a newspaper. I did not doubt their concern for me. But it made me impatient. I longed to be on my own, answerable to no one.

After the service I walked back ahead of the others. I heard Ray and Skelly calling after me to wait for them but I hurried on to a bend in the road and hid behind a wall until they had all gone by. I found conversations awkward. I was already drawing away from my contemporaries. I could not tell them about Emma and because I was unable to demonstrate how much more than them I knew I became irritated with what I saw as their naïvety. The common ground we had shared was crumbling away with each day that passed.

I still felt close to Phil Watson, but his kindness was almost an embarrassment. He never criticised, never seemed to disbelieve. It was not because he approved of my arrogance or endorsed my deviousness. But his view of friendship was straightforward. If someone was your mate, then you supported him. It was his form of personal patriotism: my friend right or wrong. He had finally persuaded his mother to let him cancel his piano lessons but, as a special favour to me, he would play 'Five O'Clock Whistle', his bony fingers stumbling on the keys as he plodded to the end of the piece.

I showed him Harry's letter. 'Do you reckon they dock his pay for the plates he smashes?' he said.

'Not if I know Harry.'

'Do you fancy his sort of life?'

I heard the girls giggling in the bakehouse and shook my head. A large part of what I wanted was all around me. But it was too difficult to explain. 'I want a proper job,' I said.

'Me too,' said Phil. 'I'd give anything to be a vet, but I'll never pass those exams. They go on for years.'

'You could do it.'

'Not a chance. It costs money.' He hitched up the spectacles which were constantly sliding down his nose. 'I'll be stuck here doing something boring. I'll think of you down in London.'

'I'll think of you too.'

'You'll not have time.'

'Of course I will,' I said. 'All the time in the world.'

It was not true. Just as it had happened before, time was somehow accelerating. Before I knew it I had started on next year's diary. The double period for Religious Instruction which Mr Gaskell had employed so variously became a weekly rehearsal for the School Certificate. We revised and then we corrected our revisions. We worked our way through old examination papers. We despaired.

I turned to Emma for consolation, but she too was aware of how time had speeded up. Both of us knew that I would soon be gone and the knowledge was like sand that gritted our skin as we lay side by side, sometimes making contact unbearable. One night a mousetrap which had been set in the grate went off like a pistol and when I got out of bed to inspect it I saw the small brown body pinned to the board, a drop of blood beading its nose.

I prised it free and showed it to Emma. 'Get rid of it,' she said.

'Where?'

'Anywhere. Down the lavatory.'

The house was dark. I crept down the stairs and into the bathroom. As I dropped the mouse into the lavatory bowl and pulled the chain Sister Kathleen's light snapped on. I tucked a towel round my waist and met her on the landing. Emma's door was ajar and we both saw it, like a book which has been left open to be returned to later.

'Go back to bed,' said Sister Kathleen. 'Your own bed.' Her face was pale and her hair was in braids. She looked at me with loathing. 'This has to stop,' she said. 'This wandering about. You have no special rights. You're still one of the boys here.'

'I know that.'

'You don't act as though you do.'

There was no sound from Emma's room and we both waited, watching the wedge of darkness out of the corners of our eyes. 'I can go myself,' I said. 'You don't have to stand over me.'

'Go on then,' said Sister Kathleen.

As I crossed the landing Emma came to the door of her room. We looked at each other and she nodded. 'Go on,' she said. 'Go back to bed.'

I climbed between my own cold sheets and lay there listening. There was a distant murmur of conversation but I could not distinguish any words. In the morning Emma and Sister Kathleen supervised breakfast as usual, but there was an air of constraint. Their exchanges were polite and, as far as anyone could judge, friendly. But they did not smile at each other and when I left to catch the bus I looked back through the window and saw them sitting on opposite sides of the table like strangers.

That evening Emma beckoned me into the sitting room. 'I told you it had to stop,' she said. 'Now you know I was right.'

'What did Kathleen say?'

'It doesn't matter what Kathleen said.'

'Is she going to tell?'

Her eyes glistened. 'Of course not. Kathleen's my friend. But it has to stop. You must understand that. It's making everyone miserable. It's wrong.'

'It's not wrong.'

'Isn't it? How did you feel out there on the landing? Were you proud of yourself? Were you proud of me?'

'You sound like my mother,' I said.

Emma straightened her shoulders and the blue silk dress tightened over her breasts. 'Perhaps it's time I did.'

I could almost hear a faint click as though somewhere a key had been turned in a lock and security restored. I could not muster any argument. I did not even want to argue. Emma had decided for us both and simultaneously I felt resigned and grateful. For the sake of appearances I blustered for the last time. 'You might change your mind.'

'I won't,' said Emma.

'Wait and see.'

She clasped my hands and held them tightly. 'Don't be silly,' she said.

After that the atmosphere lightened. I worked with new enthusiasm and with the rest of my form I sat for the School Certificate examination. It seemed to me inconceivable that I might have passed. The papers, we told each other, had never been so stiff. Phil Watson was especially gloomy. 'I'll never be a vet now,' he said. 'I sent back a blank paper for biology. Whoever set those questions ought to be shot.'

His mother rapped the top of his head so that his spectacles shot down his nose. 'And how did you manage?' she asked me.

'Just the same. I'll never pass.'

'Have you told your mother that?' asked Mrs Watson.

'More or less.'

'She'll be upset.'

'She was a teacher. She knows what it's like.'

'That won't stop her being upset.'

I was not looking forward to seeing my mother. Mr Rome had arranged for me to stay at a hostel in London – the same one to which he had sent Harry Barnes – while I learned shorthand and typing. But there was no room for me until the late summer and there were several weeks to go.

'You have to face it,' said Emma. 'You'll have to go home. Your mother's expecting you. She'll want you there when the examination results come out.'

I thought of the Potteries baking beneath the August sun and my mother sluicing soapy water over the greenfly that infested the roses. 'She'll keep on at me about London.'

'I expect she will,' said Emma. 'But there's nothing she can do about it. You're going and that's that.'

'Will I see you there?'

'When you're settled in. Just as a friend.'

'I'll be staying near Sadie,' I said.

'I know you will. I've been there, don't forget.' She smiled ironically. 'There'll be no hanky-panky while you're in that hostel. No visitors after nine o'clock. You'll have to mind your P's and Q's.'

'I've managed before.'

'Hark at him,' said Emma. She ruffled my hair. 'Just you try keeping to the rules. I don't want you shipped back here.'

She was not dismissing me; I was being released. If I closed my eyes I could recall every dip and bias of her body, but the memory no longer made me giddy with lust. It was like remembering a stretch of country with its hills and pastures, its sudden heat and its marshy scents. Without any map or compass I could give directions. I had been there. I wondered if she thought of me in the same way but I could not ask her; our relationship had altogether changed. We were intimates but we were also shy with each other. Emma had not told me what she and Kathleen had said that night on the landing. One day I supposed she would. But, for the time being, I did not want to know. I was afraid to sound an alarm which might halt the machinery which was slowly cranking up the door through which I would walk free.

Skelly helped me to choose my going-away outfit. 'The good stuff's in here,' he said, unlocking a cupboard at the back of the storeroom. 'Most of it's pre-war. You can tell by the quality.'

I picked out a brown sports jacket, grey flannels and a pair of brogues which squeaked as though they were hinged with rust. 'Are they all like this?' I asked.

'Pretty well.' Skelly ticked off my new acquisitions on his list. 'You get two shirts, two vests, two pairs of underpants, three pairs of socks and a raincoat.'

'Handkerchiefs?'

'Half a dozen. And a tie.' He saw me frown at the selection and shrugged. 'I know they're bloody awful but I didn't buy 'em. Be advised and have the lot. There's always someone ready to take it off your hands. Cash. No coupons.'

He was already versed in the customs of the world I was about to enter. 'You mean the black market?'

'That's a daft name for it.'

'The people who call round the back in those vans?'

'People like that,' said Skelly. 'I sell them some bits and pieces. Nothing fancy. I'm just getting my hand in. I'm not spending my life in someone else's storeroom. If you're crafty you can make your pile. You just have to pick your moment.'

I had never thought of Skelly having ambitions as I did. 'Don't get caught,' I said.

He rummaged in a drawer and came out with a white rayon scarf, slippery to the touch and tasselled at each end. 'Here you are. This'll make you look flash.'

'Thanks,' I said. I knotted it round my neck and stuffed my clothes into a cardboard carton. 'How long before you're off?'

'Two or three months. I might have something going for me by then.' He double-locked the cupboard and tested the door. 'There's a bloke in Bolton wants me to work for him.'

'The bloke with the van?'

'Lots of people have vans,' said Skelly. 'It doesn't mean anything. It's just business.'

I remembered an expression from a gangster film we had seen together. It had so delighted us that we had adopted it as a catch-phrase. 'Take it easy,' I said. 'But take it.'

Skelly puffed on an imaginary cigar and tapped away the ash. 'Sure thing,' he agreed.

On the morning I was due to leave Mr Rome came to Franklin House to say goodbye. Rain had fallen overnight and the lustre of his shoes was dimmed by a spattering of mud. He studied them carefully, seemingly absorbed in what he saw. 'Remember your prayers,' he said. 'Sometimes I think we pay too little heed to the spiritual welfare of the boys and girls at this branch. It's right that we should concentrate on education and jobs. But while we improve the body we must never neglect the soul.'

'Yes sir,' I said.

'I'm sure you think I'm spouting nonsense,' said Mr Rome. 'Just trotting out the old sermon. But it has to be said. It's the most important part of my job.'

I did not respond and he picked at the mud with his fingernail. 'Do you know what I'm talking about?'

'I think so, sir.'

'Does it make any impression?'

'Yes sir.'

'I wonder,' said Mr Rome. One of his toe-caps was almost clean and he blew at it to disperse the remaining dust. 'You were a problem,' he said. 'I don't mind admitting it. I had no idea what to do with you. Then Sister Emma came to the rescue. I think we should both be grateful.'

'I am, sir.'

Mr Rome stroked his nose and plucked gently at the hairs that grew at its tip. 'I'd judge the experiment to have been a success.'

'Me too, sir.' I felt myself blushing and willed the colour to subside.

'It's difficult being a guinea-pig,' said Mr Rome. 'I appreciate that. But I think everyone did their bit. Now all we have to look for are the examination results. In two weeks time, isn't it?'

'That's right, sir.'

'Can we afford to be optimistic?'

'I've no idea, sir.' I wished he would end his homily. My feelings of guilt were rapidly being overtaken by a sense of triumph so powerful that I wanted to shout aloud. I had not been found out. My secrets were still intact. Even as I congratulated myself I knew that it was unworthy, but I felt my face bend into a stupid and uncontrollable grin. I bit my lip but it would not go away. The room was suffused by light as the sun broke through the clouds and I welcomed it as an omen.

'I shall pray for you,' said Mr Rome and shook my hand.

Emma came with me to the bus stop. Before we left the house she gave me a small tissue-wrapped box and watched me peel away the paper. It contained a silver cigarette case, curved to fit into my hip pocket. 'It's lovely,' I said.

'Don't smoke too much.'

'I can't afford to.'

'You'll make your fortune one day,' said Emma. 'Make time for other things too.'

The bus was already waiting when we reached the stop. As the driver switched on the ignition I heaved my suitcase on to the top step. 'All aboard,' called the conductor and I kissed Emma goodbye. I had no doubt that Sister Beryl was watching from her bedroom in Mosscrop House, but I did not care.

'Send me a card when you get to London,' Emma said.

I backed up the steps. 'First thing.'

'And be nice to your mother.'

'I'll try.'

I sat down and the bus bore me away. I saw Mr King leading a gang of boys towards the Shop and when I waved they saluted me with their spades. The sun was stronger now and the slate roofs of the houses were drying from black to dove grey. We passed the school and then Argyle House. The plantation where I had met Sadie was in full leaf, dripping after the night's rain. I looked through the back window and watched the moors unroll behind me. Clouds and the shadows of clouds pursued us. We turned the corner and accelerated down the hill and in both directions I could see only the road, steaming under the bright sky.

I caught the Northern Flier heading south and I was at home by mid-afternoon. My mother had a headache and was lying down, but she got up to greet me, her cheeks patched with red, her eyes glittering with fever.

'You should be in bed,' I told her.

'It's an occasion. You're not often home. I can't be poorly on special days.'

'You'll just make yourself worse.'

'This is nothing,' she said, clutching the corner of the sideboard, a sharp protuberance against which I always bruised my hip when I hurried into the room. 'You've never seen me when I'm really bad.'

It was half boast, half entreaty, but I would rise to neither. Arguments with my mother, even those begun with the best of intentions, always ended in someone being hurt. It was better to remain noncommittal. 'I'd like to see you better,' I said.

It was the wrong reply. She held on to the sideboard and faced me squarely. 'You would if you were here.'

I remembered Emma's final injunction and held my tongue. 'Wouldn't you?' she persisted.

'I suppose I would.'

'You should say what you mean.'

'And you should be back in bed,' said Mary from the kitchen.

My mother swung round, almost losing her balance. 'I don't need your advice.'

'You need something, that's for sure,' said Mary.

'Let's not quarrel,' I said. 'I didn't come here for that.'

'I don't know why you did come,' said my mother. 'You needn't have bothered.'

Every day was the same. For a week I went to stay near Birmingham with my mother's school friend Zillah and her husband George. He was a dentist and a member of the Communist Party, but he preferred to talk to me about jazz and dance bands. He was an admirer of the Mills Brothers and played me their records on a wind-up gramophone, easing each one out of its brown paper envelope and wiping it with a duster before fitting it on to the turntable. His favourite was 'Smoke Rings' and he joined in the harmonies, alternating between tenor and bass, beating time with a cigarette clamped between the tawny fingers of his right hand. I imagined the same fingers probing my mouth and wondered if the patients ever complained.

I went home the day that the School Certificate results were published and telephoned Phil Watson from the house next door. 'Congrats,' he said, 'you've passed. Credits in Eng. Lit., History and Art.'

'How about you?'

'Squeaked through,' he said. 'I feel sick as a dog.'

'Still, you've passed.'

'Only just. I'll never get to be a vet.'

'Of course you will.'

'I won't,' said Phil. 'I'll be stuck here like I said.' I thought of the bakehouse smells and the girls shimmying beneath their overalls and the attic bedroom hung with film-star photographs and the comfort that contained the house like a tea-cosy and I wished that we could simply change places.

'It'll be all right,' I said. 'You'll get what you want.'

'I wouldn't bank on it.'

'Roll on,' I said. 'Something'll turn up.'

It was poor consolation and I knew it. We promised to write to each other and said goodbye. The world was filling up with farewells but this time it was me that was in motion. If I thought about it too hard my heart began to race. I composed myself and went to tell my mother the good news.

'I'm pleased,' she said. 'Mind you, I expected no less. You come from a brainy family. Look at your uncles.'

'It was me that did the work,' I said.

'The background always helps.'

'I hadn't noticed,' I said. 'Not lately.'

'What do you mean by that?'

'Nothing. All I'm saying is that I took the examnination, not them.'

'You got no distinctions,' said my mother. 'Not even in English. I thought that would come easy to a journalist working in London.'

I left the room without answering. I refused to engage in another battle which would leave us both angry and unsatisfied. I was going to London and, as Emma had reminded me, that was that. I walked to the top of the avenue and looked down on Burslem for the last time. Smoke from the pot-banks swathed the town and the gold angel still stood on tiptoe on the Public Library. I watched a flock of pigeons circle his head like a halo. They were so far away that their wings were like flecks of light, particles which caught and returned the sun. When they disappeared into the smoke I went home to pack.

My mother let me go without protest, too morose to goad me further. I promised to write every week and to join her at Christmas. She cut and parcelled my sandwiches and stood with Mary on the top step, waving until I turned the corner into High Lane. She was as fixed in my mind as the angel and the image was still with me that night when I was shown to my room at the hostel. It was in north London, surrounded by trees which muffled the sounds of traffic, but through them I could hear the throb and shuffle of the city like a beast decked in armour, restless in its stall. I lay on my bed and wondered why I felt so lonely.

Sadie was not expecting me and when I called to see her, sent word that she was washing her hair. Half an hour later she came down to the lounge where I had been told to wait. She was wearing a towel like a turban and her eyes were pink with shampoo. 'You might have warned me you were coming.'

'I didn't know,' I said. 'I decided on the spur of the moment.'

'I was going out.'

'Who with?'

'Friends,' she said vaguely.

'What friends?'

'No one you know. People from the office.'

'I'll come with you.'

'They wouldn't interest you. They're just girls.' She propped up a hand mirror on the table and began to pencil her eyebrows. Her face was thinner than I remembered it and when she removed the towel I saw that in the front of her hair there was a narrow blond streak.

'They're all doing it,' she said. 'I thought I'd give it a try.'

She was wearing a necklace of green stones and her eye shadow was the same colour. 'You look smashing,' I said.

'Do I?'

'Really.'

'Green's my colour,' she said. 'Everyone says so.'

I watched the eyebrows take shape like antennae which she had gummed to her forehead. 'Can't we just go somewhere and have a drink?' I asked. It was like someone else's voice, I thought, pleading and uncertain.

'Not tonight,' said Sadie. 'Sorry. I can't let these people down.'

She clicked down the top on her eyebrow pencil and exchanged it for a lipstick. Her mouth bloomed in the mirror and she blotted it with her handkerchief. 'Does that make it kiss-proof?' I asked.

She stared at me hard and then gave her familiar whinny of laughter. 'What do you know about making it kiss-proof?'

'They don't just do it in London.'

'I never said they did.'

'Is that why you're doing it?'

'No it's not.'

'I don't believe you.'

She gathered her belongings together and scooped them into her handbag. 'Suit yourself.' She patted my cheek and smiled. 'Look,' she said, 'you can't just turn up without warning and expect me to come running after you. We'll see each other, but not tonight. Why don't you come round tomorrow. There's a good picture at the Astoria. I'll treat you.'

'I've got my own money.'

'You'll need it,' said Sadie. 'I've already told you, things cost a lot down here.'

I did not call to see her the next night; I was not prepared to be patronised again. But by the end of the week I felt more sure of myself and asked her to come and see *Love Story* at Finsbury Park. From the back row of the stalls we watched Margaret Lockwood as the concert pianist with only six months to live concealing the awful truth from Stewart Granger, the airman who was gradually going blind. I hated the film but Sadie said it was beautiful.

'Why couldn't she just tell him she was ill?' I demanded.

She shook her head impatiently. 'You don't understand.'

'They were both being stupid.'

'No they weren't.'

'If I knew I was going to die I'd tell you,' I said.

'That doesn't prove anything. She didn't want to make things worse for him.'

'But if he loved her he'd want to know.'

'I wouldn't,' said Sadie.'

'Why not?'

'I wouldn't want the worry.'

The argument was beyond me. I pulled her into the shadow of the bushes by the gate of the hostel and kissed her. 'It's time I was in,' she said. 'They'll be locking the door any minute.'

'You can always knock them up.'

She sniggered into her clenched fist. 'You want to watch what you're saying. Nobody wants to get knocked up.'

'I didn't mean that.'

Sadie leaned against me. 'Are you sure?'

'Positive.'

'You'd better be.'

We were back on our old footing. The back-chat had been restored, raised and bolted together like scaffolding and we walked its planks with growing confidence. Sadie kissed me again and put her tongue in my mouth.

'Who taught you that?'

'Nobody.'

'Pull the other one,' I said. Not that it mattered; not then. The important thing was that we were back together, not yet lovers but soon to be. I had no doubt about that.

'Sleep tight,' she said.

'All night.'

The front door closed behind her and I walked to my own hostel. There was a letter from Emma on the table in the front hall and I took it up to my room to read. It was no more than a note. 'In London tomorrow,' it said. 'Can we meet around five o'clock?'

She took me for tea at a Lyons Corner House where a woman wearing a long black gown played the organ. 'That's Ena Baga,' I told Emma. 'She's famous.'

'For doing what?'

'She's on the wireless.'

'Is she now?' Emma poured the tea and listened to the music. 'She's got a good ear.'

It was the first time I had seen her out of uniform and it gave me an odd feeling as though she was playing a part, or perhaps being impersonated by an actress who looked like her but was younger, less positive.

'Are you settled in?' she asked.

'More or less. I start shorthand next week. They say Pitmans is awful.'

'They always say that. It won't be so bad. You'll see.' Emma topped up the tea-pot with hot water and stirred it vigorously. 'How was your mother?'

'The same as ever. Worse if anything.'

'And Sadie?'

'She's all right. She's plucking her eyebrows.'

Emma made no comment and I wondered if she had heard what I said. 'She's plucking her eyebrows,' I repeated. 'Sister Agnes wouldn't like that.'

Emma smiled briefly. 'I suppose not.' For several minutes she sat listening to Ena Baga, then she put her cup in its saucer and pushed it to one side although it was still half full. 'Are you ready to go?'

It was unusual for Emma to leave any meal unfinished but I supposed she had other people to see. 'If you like,' I said.

She paid the bill and as we left the Corner House she took my arm. 'I've got something to tell you. That's why I came down. I didn't want to put it in a letter.'

'What's that?' I was watching a flock of starlings on the building opposite. There were hundreds of them occupying every ledge and window sill, perched wing to wing, gargling and fluting, each bird adding to the babel until, as one, they took off like a scarf that had been shaken against the sky. They fanned out in a ragged skein, then regrouped and resumed their original positions. I remembered watching them years before from my bed in the school infirmary when I had been a Bluecoat boy.

'You mustn't be upset,' said Emma, 'but I'm going to have a baby.'

I continued to watch the starlings. If the bird on the far left did not move, I promised myself, Emma's words would be unspoken. I stared through the dusk and saw it hop onto the ledge below.

'It's not really surprising,' said Emma. 'It's what happens when two people make love.'

I did not know what to say. I could not believe what was happening. Every door that I had prised open in the past few weeks slammed shut in one instant and I could not see them ever opening again. I felt lost and frightened and angry. 'Are you absolutely sure?'

'Absolutely.' She squeezed my arm. 'You mustn't worry. We'll manage somehow.'

As she spoke the starlings took to the air again. They wheeled over us, the sound of their wings filling time and space and in the gathering darkness I reached for Emma's hand, seeking comfort for the father and the child.